ISSUES FOR THE SEVENTIES

R~~~~~L
DISPARITIES

EDITED BY

HUGH INNIS

Ryerson Polytechnical Institute, Toronto, Ontario

CONSULTING EDITOR: Norman Sheffe

McGRAW-HILL RYERSON LIMITED

Toronto   Montreal   New York   London   Sydney
Johannesburg   Mexico   Panama   Düsseldorf
Singapore   Rio de Janeiro   Kuala Lumpur   New Delhi

ISSUES FOR THE SEVENTIES

REGIONAL DISPARITIES

ISBN   0-07-092942-4

23456789   AP72   987654

Printed and bound in Canada

While every effort has been made to trace the owners of copyrighted material and to make due acknowledgement, the publishers would be grateful for information enabling them to correct any omissions in future editions.

CONTENTS

ACKNOWLEDGEMENTS

Cover and page 40: Westpix from Miller Services

Cover and page 67: Robert J. Bridge from Miller Services

Cover and page 84: NFB from Miller Services

Page 4: Reprinted with permission *Toronto Daily Star*

Page 15: Canadian Press

Page 24: Reprinted with permission *Toronto Daily Star*

Page 58: Courtesy B. C. Jennings Photo

Page 74: Hans L. Blohm from Miller Services

INTRODUCTION

"Did you fight geography to make a Confederation? Then fight geography to keep a Confederation."

George Foster, 1911

Canada exists as a nation in spite of her geography. A small population on an immense land mass is strung out as a thin ribbon of settlement on the American border. Even this ribbon is broken by the Rocky Mountains and by the rocky highlands of the Canadian Shield.

Some regions seem more closely drawn to parts of the United States than to other parts of Canada. The industrial province, Ontario, forms part of a great North American industrial complex surrounding the Great Lakes; British Columbia is drawn to Washington, Oregon, and California; Montreal looks to New York.

We cannot change geography. There is nothing that can be done about the fact that Canada's regions are divided by geographic barriers or by the fact that we share the North American continent with the richest, most powerful country in the world.

Confederation was a political arrangement which it was hoped would overcome geography by uniting a number of separate areas in a federal system. In our federal system there were bound to be tensions between the federal government and the provincial governments. These tensions have been heightened because the provinces are quite different from one another and view the federal government differently. Poor provinces have had a centralist view of confederation because they needed the subsidies which a strong federal government could provide. Only with assistance could they hope to have a standard of living even close to that of Ontario or British Columbia. Rich provinces have been reluctant to see tax money taken by the federal government which they felt they had earned and needed to pay for public services such as education. The federal compromise which is Canada has never been successful in working out financial terms which would help the poor provinces and gain the sympathy and understanding of the rich.

The Maritimes were reluctant to enter Confederation in 1867, and over 100 years later they are still bitter about arrangements which leave them economically so much poorer than Ontario or British Columbia. The Prairie provinces, devastated economically by the weaknesses of their wheat economy in the 1930s, still do not feel they are well served by our federal system. Economic

1

inequality helps to breed social and cultural divisions in a country already divided by geography.

Since World War II, the divisions between Canada's regions, never success-fully bridged, have widened under tremendous economic, political, and social pressure from the United States. We even regard this pressure differently in different parts of Canada. Ontario can afford to be concerned about American domination. Other parts of Canada need the economic development which American money can provide, although they are aware that the money which provides jobs also erodes Canadian identity. The nineteenth-century task of joining provinces in national unity has been made much more difficult in the twentieth century by the growing shadow of the United States.

H.I.

Part 1

Canada is a nation of rich and poor provinces. Although all the provinces have grown economically, the relative positions of the provinces in terms of income have not changed in forty years. While the average Maritimer is better off, he is as far behind the average person in Ontario as he was in the 1930s.

Since the depression, numerous meetings between federal and provincial governments have been held and numerous proposals to lessen regional disparities have been put forward. These meetings and proposals have provided us with a continuing analysis of the problem, but they have not solved it.

4

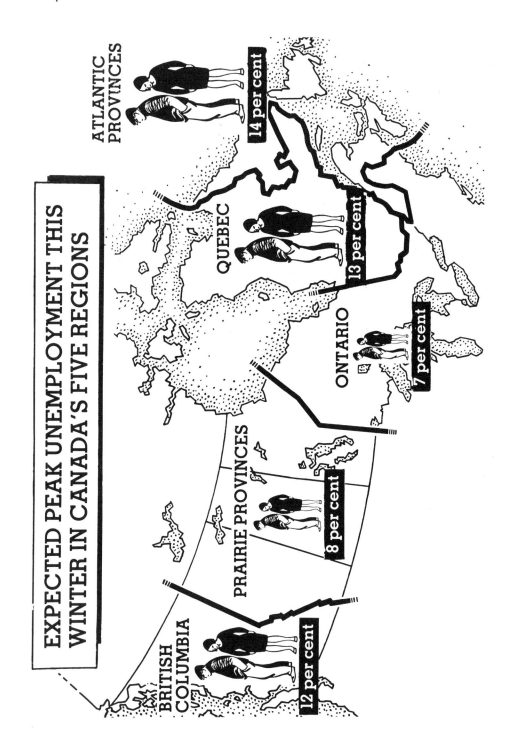

EXPECTED PEAK UNEMPLOYMENT THIS WINTER IN CANADA'S FIVE REGIONS

BRITISH COLUMBIA — 12 per cent

PRAIRIE PROVINCES — 8 per cent

ONTARIO — 7 per cent

QUEBEC — 13 per cent

ATLANTIC PROVINCES — 14 per cent

WE ARE FIVE DIFFERENT ECONOMIC NATIONS AND WE'RE IN TROUBLE

Robert Nielson

Robert Nielsen is the Editor-in-Chief of the Toronto Daily Star.

After a century of striving to pull itself together, Canada is still not so much one nation in the economic sense as five distinct and unequal regions.

Since a good picture is reputed to be worth a thousand words, let me spare you that much wordage right now by pointing to the special map. Based on a consesus of economics experts interviewed this week, it shows how unevenly the blight of unemployment will fall on Canadians this winter, according to where they live.

It explains why premiers from the Atlantic provinces, unusually abetted by the premier of Quebec, feel obliged to bore the nation with lectures on "regional economic disparities" at federal-provincial conferences. They do it for the good of our smug Ontario souls and in the hope of refreshing their treasuries with more Ottawa money.

But why does Premier W. A. C. Bennett always wear a carefree grin at these discussions? British Columbia is going to be a close third in the grim parade of the jobless this winter — a winter that is likely to see more Canadians out of work than at any time since the Great Depression. It will be a winter to shake even Ontario's prosperous complacency, for this province is heading towards a peak unemployment of 7 per cent of its labor force. Yet Ontario's worst is about what Quebec and the Atlantic provinces experience at their best times, and is only half as bad as *their* worst.

Times like this revive the ancient suspicion, East and West, that Confederation was rigged economically to enrich Ontario at the expense of the rest of the country.

Professor Rodrigue Tremblay, University of Montreal economist, has assembled data to support this thesis in a new book whose title offers his solution: *Independence and a Common Market between Quebec and the United States.* Dr. Tremblay finds that Ontario has 68 per cent of the most tariff-protected industries in Canada whereas Quebec has only 24 per cent. What happens within these protected industries matters even more to em-

Reprinted with permission, *Toronto Daily Star*, November 12, 1970.

ployment in the two provinces. In industry after industry — breweries, distilleries, rubber, furniture, paper, containers, metals, electrical appliances, to name a few — the "value added" to these products at various stages of production is much higher in Ontario than in Quebec. Textiles and tobacco are among the rare exceptions. The more value added, the more the stages of production, the more different kinds of productive facilities — in short, the more jobs. And they are generally stabler and higher-paying jobs than in the predominantly raw-materials and partly processing industries of Quebec.

Calamitous decline

Dr. Tremblay also notes a calamitous decline in Quebec's share of job-creating capital investment compared to Ontario and to Canada as a whole. For 1970 the total of private and public investment forecast for Quebec is $3.4 billion compared to $7.1 billion in Ontario. Quebec, with a population four-fifths of Ontario's is getting less than half as much capital investment. And with 29 per cent of Canada's population, Quebec is getting only 19 per cent of total Canadian investment. Six years ago, Quebec was getting 75 per cent as much investment as Ontario and 26 per cent of the Canadian total. Quebec added only a paltry 3,000 jobs this year while 75,000 new people were entering its labor force; Ontario, in a slack year, added 49,000 jobs.

This gap in investment and jobs has widened so recently and so drastically that it cannot be wholly blamed on Ontario's favored position in Confederation. It undoubtedly owes something to separatist and terrorist activity scaring away business. It also owes something to Ontario's popula-

tion being, on the average, more educated and better skilled than Quebec's. And once such a trend sets in, it accelerates because capital is so much more mobile than labor. Capital moves readily to Ontario, where the action is; labor follows, but much more slowly, especially from Quebec, where the departing worker and his family are likely to be saying farewell to their language and culture as well as their friends and familiar surroundings.

Whatever the reasons, Ontario has gained a terrific economic momentum while Quebec is faltering. This has turned the competition between the two biggest provinces into a no-contest, and it is hardly surprising that Dr. Tremblay wants out in the hope of finding a happier future for Quebec within the U.S. orbit.

Ontario's great basic strength is further underlined by a recent report of the Dominion Bureau of Statistics which attempted to measure trade flows between the different regions of Canada just as if they were five distinct nations. The bureau's figures show that in manufacturing, Ontario has a big surplus in trade with each of the other regions. In 1967, Ontario shipped $668.5 million worth of manufactured goods to the Atlantic provinces which sent only $114.3 million of manufactured goods to Ontario. Ontario's shipments to Quebec were $2.6 billion; Quebec's shipments to Ontario, $2.1 billion. To the prairie provinces Ontario sent $1.5 billion worth of manufactures and received $250.8 million worth; it shipped $747.4 million worth to British Columbia and received $121.4 million worth of B.C. goods. Since exports make jobs for our own people while imports make jobs for "foreigners," it's easy to see who gains the most employment from interprovincial trade. Of course, the other provinces make up their "deficits" in part by shipping foodstuffs, raw and partly processed materials to Ontario; but these lines of production, being often dependent on the vagaries of international markets and subject to seasonal fluctuations, are less steady employment sources than manufacturing.

It should not be overlooked that Ontario does a lot of paying-back to the rest of Canada through the excess of federal taxes collected in this province over what Ottawa spends here. This revenue "surplus" finances most of the hundreds of millions of dollars in equalization grants which Ottawa distributes to less wealthy provinces, as well as the regional development programs aimed at lifting their employment and incomes up to the national average.

In the Atlantic provinces — long handicapped by remoteness from markets, aging population, and deficiencies in education and skills — these programs and the strenuous efforts of the provincial governments to industrialize are at last beginning to show some results. Although the 14 per cent peak unemployment indicated for the Atlantic region this winter is no matter for congratulations, economists believe it would be much worse — perhaps 18 to 20 per cent — without the special, federally assisted development programs of the last decade.

Prairie slowdown

The 8 per cent unemployment expected in the prairie region — low in relation to three other regions, high in relation to its own norm — probably masks a large amount of winter underemployment. And the figure doesn't count all the farmers sitting around waiting to sell some grain. There's not much doing on the Prairies after those Arctic winds start to blow, and that's especially true this year.

All Canada's regions are peculiar, but British Columbia seems even more economically peculiar than the others. Here is a giant province whose resources and manufacturing sectors are both rapidly expanding, with a well-educated population and the highest average income in Canada among those who work. Yet its unemployment is consistently higher than the national average and, at an expected 13 per cent peak this winter, will vie with Quebec and the Atlantic provinces for the worst record. Internal transportation is difficult and expensive because of the mountains, and there's high seasonal unemployment in primary industries, but the only particular reason which the Economic Council of Canada advances for B.C.'s current ills is a rash of industrial strife.

The wide regional differences in current and expected unemployment suggest how unsatisfactory, for such a chequered country, are the across-the-map fiscal and monetary restraints which the Trudeau government has been applying. The stimulus of special programs for regions that need them is offset by the depressing effects of high interest rates and taxes. And the bottom appears to be dropping right out of the Quebec economy. If this isn't remedied in a way that produces jobs for young Quebeckers in particular, no amount of wisdom and strength from Pierre Trudeau and Robert Bourassa in the political management of the situation will keep the Quebec crisis from getting much worse.

Ottawa's strategy for depressed regions now emphasizes the "growth points" approach of the regional development minister, Jean Marchand; existing centres of industry and population are reinforced in the expectation of a fallout of economic benefits within a wide radius. Canada's regional unemployment map shows how far this program has still to go.

REGIONAL GROWTH AND DISPARITIES

The Economic Council of Canada

The legislation establishing the Council refers to the broad goals of a high and consistent rate of economic growth and a sharing by all Canadians in rising living standards. Regional participation in rising living standards is obviously an important aspect of this latter goal, and our terms of reference specifically direct us "to study how national economic policies can best foster the balanced economic development of all areas of Canada".

This concern for regionally balanced economic development, consistent with rapid growth for the country as a whole, is easily understood. Even fairly small industrial countries, possessing only limited land area and closely integrated national economies have experienced significant interregional disparities in growth and levels of income. In Canada, the physical immensity of the country, the presence of distinct geographic barriers, a narrow, uneven chain of settlement, and a striking diversity of resources and economic structure among our major regions all make for a particularly high degree of regional differentiation. It is not surprising, therefore, that the problem of integration and balance, in the sense of assuring an appropriate participation on the part of each region in the over-all process of national economic development, has long been an elusive goal and a continuing concern of the people of Canada . . .

Interregional Income Disparities

The best available statistical measure of interregional income disparities in Canada is the flow of personal income within each of the ten provinces. Personal income is the flow of income to individuals, and since by far the greater part is earned by the productive factors of labour and capital, it also provides an approximate indication of the level of economic output produced in each region. Per capita personal income is also a meas-

Reproduced with the permission of Information Canada from the Economic Council of Canada's *Second Annual Review*, pages 99-103, 136-138, *Fifth Annual Review*, pages 103, 108, 112, 121.

ure of comparative productivity and economic welfare per person among the separate regions. Thus the more closely bunched are the regional averages around the national average, the smaller is the degree of income disparity among the regions and, in our terms, the more balanced is the participation of the various regions in national economic development.

The regional levels of personal income per capita are shown for three groups of years in Table 5-1. The most striking feature of the comparisons is the substantial percentage difference in income levels between the highest and lowest province. For the recent period 1963 personal income per capita in Ontario was about four-fifths larger than in Prince Edward Island and twice that of Newfoundland. As for the other provinces, income levels in British Columbia and the Prairies are considerably above the average for all provinces; Quebec's per capita income is fairly close to the average. All the Atlantic Provinces range well below personal income per capita in the country as a whole.

A second feature of the comparisons is that the rankings of provinces in terms of income levels have hardly changed over a period of almost forty years. Ontario has changed places with British Columbia as the highest and second highest income provinces. Manitoba and Saskatchewan have also traded positions in the centre of the rankings and Quebec has maintained a consistent mid-position. The Atlantic Provinces have been at the bottom of the range throughout. The broad geographical distribution over time is also noteworthy. Income levels in the five western-most provinces have been generally higher than the provincial average since 1927 while those in eastern Canada have been lower. Moreover, while there has been some reduction in the *percentage* range of income differences, particularly with reference to peaks in disparity experienced during the early 1930's and early 1950's, the degree of disparity remains obviously large. . . . Differences in average incomes between the United States and Canada . . . are also of interest. As will be seen in Table 5-2, only the Ontario and British Columbia regions have achieved levels of personal income per capita higher than the lowest regional grouping in the United States, the seven states comprising the Southeast.

TABLE 5-1—LEVEL OF PERSONAL INCOME
PER CAPITA BY PROVINCE
(In current dollars)

	1927	1947	1963
Ontario	509	981	2,025
British Columbia	535	980	1,966
Alberta	509	923	1,750
Saskatchewan	449	818	1,749
Manitoba	455	875	1,721
Quebec	378	709	1,521
Nova Scotia	299	676	1,302
New Brunswick	277	609	1,167
Prince Edward Island	248	477	1,115
Newfoundland			1,009
Average for Provinces	**407**	**783**	**1,532**

NOTE: Provinces are ranked in order of level of personal income per capita in 1963, and the data are for three-year averages centred on the year shown. Data for British Columbia include the Yukon and Northwest Territories.
SOURCE: Based on data from Dominion Bureau of Statistics.

TABLE 5-2—CANADA AND UNITED STATES REGIONAL PER CAPITA INCOMES AS PERCENTAGE OF UNITED STATES AVERAGE, 1963
(Average for U.S. Regions = 100)

Canada		United States	
Ontario	83	Far West	118
British Columbia	80	Mid-East	116
Prairies	71	New England	112
Quebec	62	Great Lakes	107
Atlantic	47	Great Plains	95
		Rocky Mountains	94
		Southwest	85
		Southeast	74

NOTE: Calculated from data expressed in current Canadian and United States dollars.
SOURCE: Based on data from Dominion Bureau of Statistics, and U.S. Department of Commerce.

Aspects of Interregional Disparity

Despite variations in personal income per capita from region to region, the feature which emerges most strikingly from the record of the past four decades is the essential persistence of income disparity among the regions of Canada. The spread in average per capita incomes among the major regions is fairly constant throughout; and the position of each region relative to the average was virtually the same in 1926 as in 1964.

Furthermore, there is some evidence to suggest that persistence in interregional income disparity can be traced back even further in Canadian history.

Per capita income levels in the Atlantic Region have ranged below 75 per cent of the average for Canadian regions throughout the period, except for the years towards the end of World War II. After 1946, income levels in the region fell away from the average, and the inclusion of Newfoundland in the data for the Atlantic Region since 1949 has somewhat lowered the average level of income shown for that region. At the other extreme, Ontario and British Columbia have recorded income levels roughly 25 per cent above the regional average for most of the period. Per capita income in the Prairies shows an extremely wide swing away from the average during the early 1930's, reflecting the particularly adverse impact of the depression upon incomes in this region. Throughout the period, personal income per capita in Quebec has been below the regional average but, since the end of the war, the gap has been steadily narrowed.

The experience of the United States is in sharp contrast to that of Canada. . . . Most striking is the steady and significant convergence in the interregional spread of incomes since the early 1930's. Data going back well into the 19th century suggest that the narrowing process experienced in the United States is a long-standing feature of regional economic development in that country. It has been associated with the regional dispersal of growth capacity so as to embrace southern areas which traditionally had been outside the mainstream of economic advance.

(In the same report the Council analyzed some of the factors behind differences in personal income.)

The Atlantic Provinces

Although there are important distinctions among them, the four Atlantic Provinces clearly constitute the region with the lowest levels of income per capita in Canada and the area which has participated least adequately in over-all national economic growth. In this sense the Atlantic Region is the "underdeveloped region" of Canada, with a particularly unfavourable set of economic circumstances and characteristics.

First, the proportion of its population normally engaged in productive activity is lower than in other areas of the country. This fact alone would appear to account for roughly half of the gap in income per person between the region and the Canadian average. Contributing to this lower utilization of manpower resources are such factors as a relatively smaller proportion of total population in the working age group of 15-65 years, lower rates of participation in the labour force, higher than average unemployment, and relatively severe seasonal unemployment.

Second, the picture is no more favourable as regards earnings per person employed. The general educational level of the labour force is below that of other regions, and 'a larger proportion of the population live and work in rural areas where incomes are typically lower than in urban areas. Over the post-war period for which data are available, the rate of capital investment per capita has been well below the Canadian average; while regional public expenditure on growth-related services, including education, health, transport and resources development, has been consistently and substantially lower than in other Canadian regions. These conditions have also been reflected in high and sustained rates of out-migration of people from the area and in a rate of growth of employment slower than in the rest of Canada.

These are the symptoms of a region in a low-level "income-trap", and the breaking-out of that trap poses a formidable challenge to national policies for regionally balanced economic development.

Quebec

Income levels per person in Quebec fall somewhat below the average for Canada. This is similarly true of most of the other economic characteristics broadly outlined in our analysis. Manpower utilization is about 5 per cent below the national level, mainly because of lower than average participation in the labour force and higher than average unemployment. Earnings per employed person also fall about 7 per cent below the average for all regions. It is not easy to isolate the basic contributing causes but lower levels of educational attainment in the labour force and a longer run lag in investment in both the private and public sectors of the regional economy undoubtedly have played a part. It is also true that to a greater extent than in most of the other provinces, Quebec faces a difficult problem of securing subregional balance. Regional disparities within the province present a sharply contrasting picture. On the one hand, rapid cumulative growth is centred upon the large, metropolitan complex of Montreal, while on the other hand there are extensive areas of slower development comparable to the circumstances of the Atlantic Region.

In terms of regional income growth, however, Quebec's performance has been well above the average for Canada. Indeed, since 1950, rising levels of income per person in this province have been a powerful force in reducing interregional income disparity in Canada. Employment has grown almost as rapidly as in Canada as a whole. Internal migration from rural to urban areas and occupations has also been an important factor in the over-all development of Quebec's economy, especially in the post-war period.

Manitoba and Saskatchewan

These two Prairie Provinces have important distinguishing features. They are essentially similar, however, with respect to income levels and related economic characteristics, in which they rank somewhat above the average for Canada. Manpower utilization is at or above the national level, because participation in the labour force is relatively high while the rate of unemployment is the lowest in the country. Seasonal unemployment associated with agriculture, however, is large. Indeed the importance of agriculture in both economies, but particularly in Saskatchewan, is an overriding influence which affects their economic status in relation to the other regions.

Earnings per employed person average close to the national level, although relatively high concentration of employment in agriculture exerts a general downward pull. The shift out of this primary industry has involved a substitution of capital for labour on the farm and high rates of migration, both to urban areas and to other provinces. Educational attainment in the labour force approximates the national average. Rates of investment per capita have been favourable, and in Saskatchewan particularly the development of new mineral resources has diversified the productive capacity of the province. In these ways productivity and income per capita have been successfully maintained at or above the Canadian average. Nevertheless, total regional income and employment have increased relatively slowly, because a highly mobile population has been attracted away by superior employment alternatives in the most rapidly expanding areas of the country. Consequently, a more rapid and sustained rate of regional growth and participation in national economic development will depend upon the provision of suitable employment opportunities involving high productivity and income within these regions.

Ontario, Alberta and British Columbia

Only a brief discussion is required for the three remaining regions — Ontario, Alberta and British Columbia. Although all three have clearly distinguishable economic characteristics, they have maintained a consistent standing at or near the top of the regional ranking of personal income per capita in recent decades. Manpower utilization is higher than average in Ontario and Alberta, with favourable population age structures, high labour force participation rates and low unemployment. These factors are less favourable in British Columbia, but their effects are offset by the exceptionally high rate of earnings per person employed — 19 per cent greater than the national average.

In all three provinces, educational attainment in the labour force and educational investment are advanced, and rates of new investment have been well above average. In the range of factors whose impact we have not been able to measure statistically — resource endowment, scale of enterprise and the stimulus of urban agglomeration, location and the use of advanced technology — these regions are relatively more favoured than most other provinces. With all these factors contributing to their rapid growth in employment, population, and total income, these regions have clearly participated very strongly in national economic development. At the same time, to a greater extent than elsewhere, these regions have been particularly confronted with those problems associated with a sharp increase in the concentration of people and economic activity. These include specifically the problems of urban congestion, the optimum use of land, and the provision of services and facilities required to accommodate rapid urban growth. The solution to these problems clearly entails heavy capital investment and far-reaching, complex changes in the institutional framework to enable it to adapt to new needs.

CONSTITUTIONAL CONFERENCE FEBRUARY, 1969

On February 10, 1969, the second meeting of a Constitutional Conference was called to order by Prime Minister Trudeau in Ottawa. The Constitutional Conference had been originally established to examine Canada's constitution, in all its parts, in order to determine what changes, if any, might be desirable if the rights of French-Canadians were to be better protected and promoted. At this particular meeting, the provincial premiers indicated that they had many things, besides Quebec, on their minds.

Premier Smallwood put his feelings very plainly.

Prime Minister, I will be very frank and say that the matter that really bites into our vitals in Newfoundland, as I am sure it does in New Brunswick and Nova Scotia and Prince Edward Island, and possibly other parts of Canada; the thing that really is the gut issue for us in Newfoundland is this matter of economic and fiscal disparity between the provinces and between other regions of Canada, groups of provinces or even parts of one province as against other parts of the same province. This is the issue for us.

He spoke very vividly of poverty.

And people have to live generally on a lower standard, which means to say, Prime Minister, that some little youngster that is going to be born tomorrow night, or tonight, or at daylight tomorrow morning, somewhere east of that line, north-south line in Quebec, or anywhere east of that in Quebec and in the four Atlantic Provinces — some little baby is going to be born tomorrow morning of whom you may say that a Court has condemned that Canadian baby to an inferior existence, food not so good, home not so good; schools not so good, hospitals not so good, roads not so good, municipal services not so good. That child is condemned, as though a Court had done it, to an existence inferior to the Canadian average, certainly the Ontario average.

Now, is that just the responsibility of Premier Campbell? Is it just we four who have to worry about that? Isn't this something, Sir, for you and the great Parliament of our great nation? Isn't it something for you and your colleagues in the Government of Can-

Reproduced with the permission of Information Canada, from the *Constitutional Conference Proceedings,* Second Meeting, February 10-12, 1969.

ada? Isn't this a concern of Ontario?

Let us look at that for a moment. Look, we can't have breakfast in the morning without paying profits to some firm in Ontario. When we get out of bed the very bed we get out of came from Ontario. The mattress and the spring came from Ontario. And the bedclothes on it came from Ontario. And when we step down on the floor the carpet, if we are rich enough, or the linoleum, or the old fashioned canvas, that came from Ontario.

Smallwood was joined by Louis Robichaud the premier of New Brunswick who spoke of poverty and of one idea which would alleviate a problem in the Maritimes. Not surprisingly the idea had to do with tariffs.

Perhaps I should thank you Prime Minister, and all the other Premiers, for the interest that they are showing in the economy of the Atlantic area for having allowed this item of regional disparities to be included on the agenda of this Conference.

Over the years you people from other parts of the Country have heard of this problem of economic disparity in our Country which affects us more perhaps than in any other part of Canada.

Over the years we argued that something dramatic should be done to alleviate the burden that the residents of the Atlantic area have to support.

Over the years successive governments and people in this Country have been listening to us with very sympathetic ears and over the years a lot of patch work, I should say, has been done.

It is most humiliating for us to *appear before this august body and before the Canadian nation and appear like beggars. We are not beggars. We do not want to be beggars. We simply want our fair share of the national wealth.*

I should say that over the years our argument was very eloquently submitted to various authorities. It was eloquently submitted yesterday by the Premier of Newfoundland, Mr. Smallwood, and we all know he is very eloquent and he can make a point when he wants to make it. . . .

Yesterday Premier Smallwood said that the per capita income in his province is approximately half that of Ontario and that is true, but he didn't say everything he could have. He didn't say everything. The per capita income of the residents, the workers or everybody in the Atlantic Provinces is half that of Ontario, but our taxes are double those of Ontario.

Now, we are Canadians and we want to remain Canadians, and over the years we have got this situation.

Perhaps there has never been a Prime Minister of Ontario as sympathetic as Prime Minister Robarts to our problems. He wants to do something about it. He wants to find a formula and we have found some sort of formula with the equalization formula, certain agencies such as FRED, ARDA, and the Hydro Development Programme.

This, I submit, is patchwork, but I would like to go back to what I was saying. Our taxes are double what they are in Ontario. In fact the municipal taxes and the provincial taxes are double. That is not all. We, for instance, buy a car in the Atlantic Provinces. Everybody has a car. It is no longer a luxury to have a car. It is a necessity of life. We buy a car which is manufactured in Ontario. We pay $300 to $400 more than the resident of Ontario has to pay for a car, just to buy it; and after that car is purchased then we have to pay much higher taxes than the resident of Ontario has to pay in taxes to operate his car.

Now, in so many areas we are — let us put it bluntly — somewhat discriminated against. Why — because of transportation problems, of course, but I am wondering if something really dramatic should not be done and now. I do not think we can wait any longer.

I do not know what the solution is but let us think for a moment of the abolition of tariffs between the United States and Canada if that were feasible, along the Atlantic border with the United States not the rest of Canada, they don't need it. If that were feasible, do you know what it would mean? It would mean that every resident of the Atlantic Provinces would save approximately $1,000 for the purchase of a car — $1,000 for the purchase of a car per citizen.

Premier Smallwood at this conference commented on a suggestion from Prime Minister Robarts of Ontario and on the promotion of industrial development.

I do not forget that in the great conference he held in Toronto, or just around that time, he made a suggestion that what appeared to be a large sum, and was a large sum, a thousand million — a billion dollars — should be set aside for the development of the economy of the four Atlantic Provinces.

That was a generous thought. It was a civilized thought. It was not enough money, but it was a kindly thought. Coming from Canada's richest Province. I have not forgotten that, and with Premier Robichaud, I agree that Mr. Robarts is a friend to the idea — or not unfriendly, I suppose, provided it does not cost Ontario too much — friendly to the idea that Canada as Canada, the Parliament, the Government of Canada as such, doing something, something more than has been done to help these four Provinces to develop their own economy; not just to be poorhouses for Canada. Still less to be poor, dependent colonies of Canada.

Incidentally, we were a colony until just 20 years ago. Twenty years ago just before the stroke of midnight, March 31st coming, we will have ceased for 20 years to be a colony. We were a colony for nearly 500 years, and we know all about it. We don't like it. We don't want to go back to that status, even to be a Canadian colony. Still less perhaps, a Canadian poorhouse. So we do appreciate what Mr. Robarts said. That is a year or so ago.

Prime Minister, a few months ago I invited a high-ranking official of our Department of Finance to travel across Canada and meet the premiers and their ministers of economics or whatever was the local equivalent of a minister of trade, industry, commerce, economics, and bring back to me in St. John's a description of what each individual province was doing, the government in each province, to attract industry to its soil.

I got an eye-opener. The first eye-opener I got was the fact that virtually all provinces across Can-

18

ada are making strenuous efforts to attract industry to their shores or to their soil. And by "strenuous efforts" I mean financial efforts, loans, cash, subsidies, subsidies of land or cash or buildings or machinery. That was my first great surprise.

My second was that the province that does most in that direction is the one that you would think least needed to do it: the great industrial heartland of this nation, the Province of Ontario.

If you want to start an industry in Canada, go first to the Premier of Ontario because from him and his administration you will get more help, more encouragement of a practical character, than you can get in any other province. That is known in Newfoundland as feeding the fat sow!

As a matter of fact, you know if you go back just a little bit, go back to the eve of the First World War — that is not terribly long ago — at that point there was not a great level of difference between Ontario on the one hand and the then remaining eight Provinces. Not a vast amount of difference. But that First World War put Ontario really on the industrial map in Canada.

She had got a flying start when the war ended and the Depression ended and then a new wave of growth started in Canada and then came the Second World War, and what that did for the industrial economy of Ontario was fantastic. It did it for some other parts of Canada at the same time, but not on the same scale, so today we have in North America here a great area and industrial empire, the empire of Ontario.

Smallwood talked about Newfound-land's efforts to promote economic development and asked for financial aid from the federal government.

We have striven mightily in Newfoundland to develop our economy. Look at the Churchill Falls. The Canadian Government helped, they helped on tax concessions, but the Newfoundland government by its efforts have brought to Canada (to Newfoundland, but that is Canada) we have brought the world's biggest and history's biggest single hydro-electric development.

I argued about that with Mr. Kosygin when he was in Newfoundland last year. I was asked to meet him officially and I went to meet him and told him about Churchill Falls. He said "How many kilowatts?" I said "I don't know, but I know how many horsepower, between 10 and 11 million horsepower on the Churchill River." He turned around and talked in Russian, or something, and they did some figuring and he said "We beat you". This discouraged me because I am proud that we have in our Province the world's biggest single hydro development. It turned out that I was right. He was talking about half a dozen put together.

We brought that to Canada, Newfoundland did.

Premier Robarts, when you give a thought to the equalization payments going to the Newfoundland government give a thought also to the fact that a thousand million dollars, a billion dollars, has been brought into Canada or is being brought in from outside Canada by this Newfoundland government to get the Churchill Falls going. That thousand million is only a part because the further development on the same river will require another thousand million. That is when you include the great transmission lines in Quebec and in Labrador. Two thousand million — this is a fair contribution to the upbuilding of Canada's industrial and economic strength. Nova Scotia does the same thing, New Brunswick does the same thing. We are making what is an important contribution to the upbuilding of the Canadian economy but it is too little and too slow, spread over too long a period of time. Meanwhile our population drops. Meanwhile the gap — in spite of our efforts, our own efforts, our own efforts and we don't spare them — in spite of these the gap widens between the four Atlantic Provinces and the big section in Quebec and the rest of Canada. This is not just our headache of us four men and our Cabinet colleagues. Surely it is your headache, Prime Minister, and the headache of your colleagues. Surely it is the concern of the whole Parliament of Canada and surely it is the concern of Canada's twenty million people that twenty per cent, one-fifth of the Canadian people, good loyal Canadians, are — not deliberately, not consciously, not purposely, or anything like that — but by lack of purpose perhaps, lack of policy, lack of programme are left almost (I don't want to exaggerate) left almost to stew in their own juices while other parts of Canada leap ahead. They do, they are leaping ahead and this is a good thing, but could we get a little leap too? Could we get a conscious deliberate acceleration of your own policy, Prime Minister? You will go down in Canadian history, I believe, for two great things. One is your noble attempt to get Canadian people all across this lovely land to agree to do the things that must be done

constitutionally to create and strengthen Canadian unity and harmony and greatness. There cannot be greatness without unity and harmony. You will go down in history, as your predecessor Mr. Pearson will too, and I think the thing that distinguishes you more than anything is your policy of having one Canada not only constitutionally but economically; not a rich Canada and a poor Canada. Not a number of "have" Provinces and some "the less you talk about the better" when you talk about wealth; and if not to end that, to reduce and to diminish it.

I have only one other thing to say and that is I happen to know that you have not got as much, you are a little short of cash and the Canadian government has not got as much money as it used to have. All the governments in Canada, the Federal Government and the ten Provincial Governments and a couple of thousand municipalities, school boards, and all kinds of public bodies in the last ten or twelve years in the aggregate have been taking simply too much money out of the Canadian economy. This is my fear. I believe they have got to hesitate and they have got to pause now for a year or so. They have reached a plateau now of public spending and from that plateau, which is a pretty high one, the highest there ever was in Canada, from that plateau these governments are looking down over the edge at the economy. I suggest we stay at that plateau or drop down a little and let the economy catch up.

It is hard to say you will put two or three hundred million into the Atlantic Provinces . . . . Could we use two or three hundred million! We will use it alone if you don't want it. If you don't want it we will use it. In Newfoundland we desperately need it.

Prime Minister, having been fair let me be something else! Your budget this year is $13.6 billion, thirteen billion, six hundred million. When you get to that size it is like when I worked in New York one time in a thirty storey building. I worked on the top floor and if you lifted your feet off the floor you would find yourself swinging. With your feet on the floor you didn't notice that. The building used to sway three or four inches and there was a total sway of six to eight inches. If you kept your feet up it soon got ahead of you. Now when you have a budget of thirteen billion six hundred million, a little creak, a little creaking of that is a couple of hundred million. If you know what I mean. Let it creak a little in our direction this year, then next year creak a little bit, then the year after that . . . .

What I am saying is I know that this is no year, I know this is not the year to look for the full implementation of the just society. It turns my stomach, really it does, to hear such a desperate violation of common sense, when you hear people say the just society has not arrived in the last six months. This is sickening. I know this year you are trying to balance the budget and stabilize Canada's economy. I know it is not the year to look for the big haul, but let us have a little haul, a little implementation of your great policy of reducing regional disparity and we will all be very happy.

Prime Minister Robarts indicated that Ontario wished to see greater equality in standards of living across Canada.

I would like to make it very clear that Ontario has always supported the principle of equalization in our Country. I did not realize all the beds in Newfoundland were made in Ontario, nor that all the breakfast food that is eaten there is manufactured in Ontario, but we do realize and understand full well that Ontario's prosperity is based on a whole range of factors. Some of them are just the luck of geography, some of them are the gift of God, and some just the fact that we happen to be part of that great country called Canada.

We recognize this and we are at all times prepared to do our part in ensuring that we have something at least approaching minimum standards across Canada. There must be some meaning to being a Canadian regardless of where you live, regardless of the economic circummstances of the particular area in which you live. This is a very fundamental and a very basic problem.

Mr. A. R. Donahue the Attorney General and Minister of Health for Nova Scotia felt that greater economic equality among provinces should be built into Canada's constitution.

We do not suggest that the regions have no responsibility for helping themselves. On the contrary, we believe that they have the duty to help themselves in every way they can, and just as far as their own resources will permit. But we do believe that the question of regional disparity and the manner of dealing with it falls into two parts: the first part is that if we are to avoid regional disparity we must arrange a system by which government is able to provide services to its people at the uniform level across the country. And the second part of the problem of regional disparity relates to economic growth and development.

As to the first part we hold it to be the right of Canadians in every region of Canada to have a standard of public services equal to the national average without a burden of taxation greater than the national average burden, and this takes us, of course, into the area of equalization.

We believe that the principle of equalization and the formula for it should be set out in the Constitution. There should be no arguing and bargaining for equalization from time to time. It should not depend upon the attitude or the whim of any particular administration at any given moment.

A formula for full equalization should, in our opinion, be part of the Constitution, and the formula for full equalization should be agreed upon.

Full equalization should contain proper allowances for municipal tax-raising ability and expenditure responsibilities. Such municipal factors are not included in the present formula. The federal representatives at the time the present equalization formula was adopted did not dispute that the formula was in fact incomplete without taking into account municipal factors. Indeed the Minister of Finance at the time agreed — categorically agreed — that these factors were excluded only because it would cost more money to include them than he was prepared to say that the Federal Government would find at that time.

As to the second aspect of the disparity problem, economic development, we hold that Canadians in every region of Canada clearly should have opportunities for their own all-round development, and to attain a standard of living reasonably comparable with the opportunities and standards of the average Canadian.

We believe that this as a compulsory general objective of federal policies should be recognized by the Constitution. There should also be written in the Constitution a provision that the Federal Government must apply its fiscal monetary and economic policies — and I say this in all seriousness — with due regard for the probable effect of each policy upon each region, and in a manner as little detrimental to the growth of each region as is consistent with the overall objective of the policy.

As they had in the 1930's, representatives from the Maritimes and the western provinces spoke about tariffs. The Premier of Alberta, Harry E. Strom, said, in part,

The economy of the West is based to a very large degree upon the production of certain raw resources. We are endeavouring to develop secondary industries, but no matter how much secondary industry we acquire, the specific raw resource industries will continue to be the base of the Western economy, and our primary contribution to the national economy.

The growth of these industries is beyond the control of regional government, though to some extent within the control of the Federal Government. I refer especially to national transportation policy and to tariff regulations.

This need not be a bad situation if it were not for the fact that when Westerners examine the Federal Government's priorities in industrial development, the order which they see is the following: the manufacturing industries in Eastern and Central Canada, the raw resource industries of Eastern and Central Canada, then, the raw resources industries of Western Canada and finally, the manufacturing industries of Western Canada.

This order of priorities is not a figment of our imagination.

What Western Canadians legitimately desire, if economic justice is to prevail within Confederation, is that our raw resource industries be given the same priority as the manufacturing industries of Eastern and Central Canada.

We desire this equality of priority to be demonstrated not simply in conference communiques but in concrete ways.

For example, when the Federal Government sets tariffs we would like to give full consideration not only to the needs of certain Eastern industries for protection, but equal consideration to the fact that the costs of these tariffs are to a large extent borne by consumers and Western industries, which must compete with high production costs and high transportation costs in an international market.

It is time the Federal Government recognized the harmful effect of the tariff system on the West, and indeed on the economic health of the nation.

Thirteen years ago, Professor J. H. Young estimated for the Gordon Commission that the tariffs were costing the people of Canada one billion dollars a year.

No reliable figures on the current cost of the tariff system are available. But we have no reason to suppose the figure would be any lower.

It is true the cost of the tariff system is borne by all Canadians.

But not all Canadians benefit from it.

It was set up, as we all know, for the protection of secondary industry in central Canada, chiefly in Ontario. Very few Western industries gained any benefit from it. And most ironically, the tariff system has failed to achieve its very objective of fostering Canadian secondary industry.

A study by Professor J. H. Dales of the University of Toronto showed some time ago that despite tariffs, Canadian economic growth has lagged behind that of the United States since 1870; that the ratio of our Gross National Product to theirs has fallen; that the ratio of our secondary manufacturing to theirs is no higher now than it was in 1910.

And yet, gentlemen, one of our major industries, agriculture, has been rising in productivity compared with the United States, despite very limited tariff protection.

For us, the tariff system symbolizes the economic imbalance of Confederation.

We see the logic of protecting infant industries but some of the "infants" are now eighty years of age and we are tired of paying their pensions.

If the Federal Government is prepared to use its influence to secure entrance to foreign markets for Canadian producers, we want it to work as hard on behalf of the raw resource industries of the West . . . .

Would it be a national tragedy for Canadian consumers to be able to purchase low-cost Japanese colour television sets if it meant that some workers in Eastern Canada would have to be retrained for new jobs?

High import duties on Asian manufacturers do more than retrict imports. They reduce the amount of Canadian exchange which Asian countries have to purchase Canadian raw materials. Since the bulk of these raw materials are materials produced in the West, such policies restrict our trade and depress the standard of living of our workers.

Again as in the 1930's the provinces discussed the distribution of powers and responsibilities between the federal and the provincial governments.

Premier Bennett of British Columbia discussed the distribution of powers and the problem of economic disparity among provinces.

British Columbia suggests there are, in addition, certain matters of mutual concern for which there should be concurrent constitutional jurisdiction and shared responsibility.

Superimposed upon the distribution of powers as we envisage them, we are of the view their is a need to have within the Constitution the machinery to permit the delegation of jurisdiction between the Federal and Provincial Governments when they so desire. Such a device, which is presently lacking in the Constitution, would add an element of flexibility and accommodation so necessary in this great growing Nation.

It is almost trite to mention that the capacity of each Government to tax must be sufficient for each Government to effectively discharge its constitutional obligations. And yet the experience of the tax-sharing arrangements over the past year has shown this is a principle that seemingly is often

lost sight of, much less subscribed to.

In the light of burgeoning Provincial responsibilities, particularly in the fields of education, health, and welfare, British Columbia can see no other alternative if Provincial responsibilities are to be met than for the Federal Government to withdraw from the direct tax fields of personal and corporate income taxes and succession duties or estate taxes.

When those changes have been made, it is our view the Constitution should restrict the spending power of the Federal Government to those matters under its jurisdiction.

I want to point out, Mr. Prime Minister, that British Columbia has some difficulty in understanding the views of some Provinces who say it is all right for the Federal Government to tax the Provinces for equalization payments to others but has not the right to tax for this great social advance of medicare. I cannot understand that logic at all.

I want to emphasize that the stresses within the nation at the present time are primarily economic and financial in nature. If we are to achieve that high destiny to which I am sure all of us around this table believe Canada is called, then we must do more to bring about economic opportunity for all citizens in all regions of Canada. I want to underscore so much of what was said on this subject at the Constitutional Conference of February last. Unless the problems of the glaring discrepancies in standards of living and economic opportunities for low-income citizens wherever they may be found in Canada are met,

then the consideration of many of the matters which are being discussed during these days may prove to be little more than academic. I am not minimizing the importance of such matters as language, culture, and constitutional review generally. But I am saying, that if we are to have and develop the kind of Canada we all unquestionably desire, then the scope of our vision must embrace the economic facts of life in Canada, which call for a frank appraisal of what national policy should be adopted to improve the situation. British Columbia believes the solution lies in direct assistance to persons — to people — of low income rather than through large unconditional payments to certain Provincial Governments.

The difficulty that help to nations around the world that Canada shares— though Canada does a better job than most — is that money does not get to the people, and since within Canada we have not had any real improvement on a comparison basis since we have had equalization payments to some provinces, shows that this does not get to the root of the matter.

We would like to see a basic income for Canadians everywhere. Every person would fill out an income tax return, and those that pay taxes, that are due to pay taxes, will pay them, and those that are below that level — it will be on the basis of how many dependants they have as well — they will be reimbursed, and they will get a cheque. So there will be a two-way flow of cheques like there should be. Those that benefit greatly from our system and all that our system means pay taxes to our government, and if because of illness and sickness and bad health and bad luck and circumstances, then the state (which is all of us) lifts them up on the basis of dignity. We think that is a solution to this great problem — at least it will be a great start towards it.

Naturally, any policies to raise the standard of living of all low-income persons will benefit most those areas with the highest incidence of inadequate income. Some areas might be 40 per cent which would get money back; other areas might only be 5 per cent, and that is the way to get it to people. And if you set that floor under the economy in all Provinces, that is the way to lift their standard of living. But I would also point out, Mr. Prime Minister, that no matter what government policies of special help to individuals are involved, the real solution will come as well when we have uniform wage rates across Canada. Now, we in British Columbia realize that cannot be done overnight. But that is where we should be directing our course. Governments should start by introducing uniform minimum wages of comparable industry for all areas of Canada.

Premier G. I. Smith of Nova Scotia pointed out that regional economic problems emerged very clearly at the time of the depression.

The unity of Canada is threatened by regional disparity just as it is threatened by linguistic or cultural differences. But this threat to national unity is not new. I should like to refer you to a statement in the report of the Royal Commission on Dominion-Provincial

Relations, as it was then called, constituted by the Government of Canada in 1937 which examined the allocation of responsibilities and powers of the federal and provincial governments and the results of such allocations, and this is the quotation I wish to mention:

"More important than all these considerations taken together is the danger to national unity if the citizens of distressed provinces come to feel that their interests are completely disregarded."

Mr. Prime Minister, I should like to say a few words generally about distribution of powers. I suggest that too often we talk about powers when in fact we are talking about responsibilities of governments to the Canadian people. After all, these things we call powers are only the means whereby governments discharge these responsibilities.

I join with others in saying in our view a great deal of the trouble we are experiencing in Canada arises from the fact that the distribution of responsibilities and powers that were relatively well in balance in 1867 are no longer in balance, and indeed are far from it. Changes have altered the whole concept of the place of government in our society. Welfare, health, education and highways, for example, which in 1867 imposed little responsibility on government at any level — and certainly not at a provincial level —are today regarded as being directly the responsibility of the provincial governments, and very heavy and costly and important responsibilities they are. These responsibilities of the provincial gov-

ernments have grown, and continue to grow, but as far as the Constitution is concerned, the fiscal powers of the provinces remain unchanged. Let me quote again from the same Royal Commission I mentioned before which recognized this problem when it stated:

"It is clear that the present situation in Canadian public finance represents a wide departure from the conception of the Fathers of Confederation and from the spirit of the fiancial settlement which they devised."

This Conference is faced with fiscal difficulties and differences which are immediate and pressing. I do not minimize these differences nor the need for resolving them, but we feel we cannot emphasize too strongly that we should not and must not permit one major problem to prevent us from giving most careful consideration to all aspects of constitutional reform.

I ask you to bear with me, Sir, while I quote again another point from the report of the same Royal Commission, which although it was written some 29 years ago, expresses in very clear language the situation in which we find ourselves today:

"Canada's present and prospective economic condition makes it clear that we can neither continue to afford the friction and waste of conflicting policies, nor the greater loss due to paralysis of policy arising from a possibly obsolete division of governmental responsibilities and powers."

We believe that today that is just as true.

Part 2

To the native of the prairies Alberta is the far West; British Columbia the near East.

Edward A. McCourt, *Canada West in*
Fiction, 1949, preface.

Western Canada has paid for the development of Canadian nationality, and it would appear that it must continue to pay. The acquisitiveness of eastern Canada shows little sign of abatement.

H. A. Innis, *History of the C.P.R.,* 1923.

NOTES TOWARDS A DEFINITION OF THE MIND OF THE WEST

Or: Why the West hates the East and may well continue doing so

Arnold Edinborough

Arnold Edinborough has been a speaker, journalist, newspaper editor, publisher and broadcaster.

As long as there has been a "Western Canada," it has hated the East. And why not? Half the original Westerners were people who went there because they couldn't stand their friends and relatives back East. Many of the rest were adventurers who went there to make their fortune, did so, and then discovered that the fortune went straight back to the Eastern financiers who had grubstaked them or had somehow acquired the Western land before the Westerners got there. Wave after wave of westward immigration didn't change the resentment this produced. Great areas of prairie were broken by Ukrainians, Germans, Russians, Swedes, and others — they all helped found the West, and therefore helped found Canada. So what was all this talk about just *two* "founding races"? These non-British, non-French Westerners were also founders; they, too, had difficulties — indeed, the prairie climate was a fiercer enemy than the Indians faced by the French.

If you went West in the early days, you had to be tough. To live there you still have to be. If you aren't tough, for instance, how can you endure a Winnipeg winter? It takes a particular strain of toughness to endure a winter like the one Edmonton went through this year. There, in January, one didn't hope the thermometer would go above freezing; one prayed hard it would budge even one degree above zero.

But the Prairies aren't the whole West. While Edmonton shivers and Winnipeg is frozen solid, the grass is green in Vancouver. The grass is always green in Vancouver: so why do insensitive national advertisers, in March, fill the TV screens and the pages of national magazines with urgent demands for Canadians to buy snow tires? The reason is that it's winter in the East and the mass media are controlled in the East. Once the snow melts in Montreal and Toronto, winter is over for the mass media. But then it's still winter on the Prairies . . . .

Of such grievances — trivial, in some eyes — are national differences made. Those snow-tire ads make some West Coast people furious; they think that no one in the East

With permission of the author and of the editor of *Saturday Night* magazine, July 1969.

knows they exist, and this becomes one of the subjects of the letters to the editor they pour on the eastern media. More letters to the editor are written to Toronto by people living in British Columbia than from all other provinces combined, and not all of this is explained by the blood pressure of the inhabitants of that province. Partly it is due to lack of other business. The writers are frequently retired prairie farmers whose time hangs heavily on their hands. Their attitude contributes something important to the B.C.-versus-the East conflict. They see themselves as persons who have lived clean, sober and industrious lives in a rural setting; now they conceive of themselves as the moral guardians of civilization. They look out from their retirement and see Canadians, especially urban Eastern Canadians, wallowing in luxury, their houses full of labour-saving devices, their children full of anarchistic ideas, and their lives full of empty pleasures like drinking, eating, and sex. And what makes these pleasures especially wicked is that, as West Coast people sometimes see it, they are subsidized by the Westerners through Ottawa.

Who writes all those dirty books? Easterners. Who pays them to do so? The Canada Council. Who puts up the money for the Canada Council? Westerners, in their taxes. And not only books. What about films? The National Film Board is subsidized by all Canadians, East and West, but it has its headquarters in Montreal. The feature film industry is also to get subventions. And where do they make their films? Toronto and Montreal. Not to mention, of course, that great wen on the body politic, the CBC. Headquartered in Ottawa, its English production centre is in Toronto, its French one in Montreal.

Such squandering of public money to gratify the degraded tastes of the East is not only bad in itself, but for these television shows which nobody in the West wants to see, Western taxes are taken and the money spent in the East. Not only do the Easterners thus get the programmes they want; they are paid to produce them.

This is particularly galling for those who have always shied away from such entertainment. But it's harder still when you have retired and are living on a fixed income. Such Ottawa-engendered affluence not only decreases the value of Western dollars but takes more and more of them to pay the shot for what is causing the inflation.

It's all due to Ottawa. Ottawa. The red flag for any Western bull. Where is Ottawa? In the centre of the country? No. In the far East, on the borders of Quebec and Ontario. And Quebec and Ontario think they own it. For when Ottawa talks of Confederation, it only considers the Eastern point of view. The constitutional problems are the problems between Ontario and Quebec. Bennett can protest. Thatcher can scream, Strom can get tough and Weir can stick doggedly to his preoccupation with the total tax load. But who gets on the television screens? Who gets the ink in the papers? The premier of Quebec, for whose indisposition in the first place that last conference was postponed. Bertrand gets better and attends; Thatcher has flu and the conference goes merrily on without him.

Ottawa looks after the economics of the country with a similar Eastern bias. Western wheat is a mere pawn in a big international game. When the world needed wheat, the Ottawa government stuck to the basic price and sold it below the world market.

When demand decreased, it stuck to the world price and didn't sell any at all. When there is too much wheat we don't do deals. When there isn't enough, we don't. Either way, the Western farmer is robbed — or believes he is.

Wheat is not the only thing. All the basic materials produced in such quantity by the West — wood-pulp, lumber, minerals, oil, gas and energy — are sold on the world market at world prices. The tools with which these goods are mined, processed or grown are bought at Canadian prices — prices which reflect the tariffs imposed on imports by Eastern industry. Inefficiencies hide behind those Eastern tariff walls.

So the primary producer in the West, whose profit is not sufficient to meet capital costs as well as current expenses, has to borrow money. Where does he borrow it? From banks — *in the East*. He has no Western bank because the Easterners won't let him. The one in Winnipeg never got into business, the one in British Columbia got into business only politically.

And who finances the large new developments in the West? Even in these days of the global village, downtown development in Vancouver, Calgary, Edmonton and Winnipeg is backed by Eastern names like Eaton's, Simpson's, and (one hates to mention it, it's such a trigger for Western anger) the CPR.

All this is quite apart from the Quebec question. On Quebec, the Western attitude is very hard. I remember the Victoria man who said to me: "I don't see any problem. If there's a revolt, we just send in the troops." I asked him how he thought the Van Doos would react to the order that they shoot their fellow French Canadians. "We wouldn't send them," he replied. "We'll keep them in Cyprus and send in the RCR."

To most Westerners, anyway, the whole Quebec thing is just a lot of talk. All very quaint to want to speak French, but doesn't the continent speak English? Who are the Quebeckers to think they can put the linguistic clock back? And don't they get all sorts of special privileges now? French radio, French television, French as well as English on cereal boxes and government cheques — even a French Prime Minister. And for God's sake, what about Expo? Millions of dollars, contributed by every taxpayer in Canada to boost the business of the merchants of Montreal. We are still paying for it, even when it is now admitted that Montreal is the only city which benefits by it. As far as the average Westerner is concerned, Lévesque can take Quebec and beat it. We should lose the port of Montreal, half the St. Lawrence Seaway, a good deal of the garment industry, and much of our early history. But we should retain the Queen and we should all speak English. Isn't that a fair swap?

Nine English provinces, the argument goes, could get on much more easily with each other than the present ten.

Ah, but could they? For all the retired farmers on the West coast there are a lot of natives who are less set in their ways. It's Vancouver that has a town fool, not Ottawa. It's Simon Fraser that has had riots, not the University of Toronto, and the biggest traffic in drugs is in Vancouver, not Montreal.

So what's to do? Will the West allow its attitudes to wreck Confederation? Will its hatred of Quebec show itself so plainly that Quebec nationalism will triumph despite all the friendly gestures from Ontario?

Diefenbaker is prepared to push his Western Tories into such a position, as his vote on the language bill showed. And if that were to happen, there are industrialists who would like to see a customs union with the U.S. before they would negotiate one with a separate Quebec.

But I don't know. I'm a farmer's son, and half of the Western view seems to me to be the grumbles of any farmer, anywhere in the world. As to climate, both atmospheric and intellectual, even the most willing Easterner can't change that, and the Westerner knows it. And as to Canada — well, if there weren't the Easterner to blame for everything, the Westerner would have to blame himself when wheat wouldn't sell, or potash got beaten on the world market, or the Japanese insisted on more leeway in their development of B.C. copper and iron.

That would never do; the Westerner is not always right, but he is never wrong. Ask Premier Bennett. Ask particularly ex-Premier Manning.

You don't need to ask Ross Thatcher. He says so only too often.

So we'll carry on, one supposes, until the West becomes more urban — as it is rapidly doing. For urban development will bring an end to many of the things which now separate the East from the West. When the present generation of farmers has gone it will be replaced by one which has spent many a winter in Florida. And if one abolishes winter, if one has lived in the lap of Miami luxury, even Toronto will look austere enough to keep Confederation together.

As for Montreal; well, if Toronto can take it, so can the West. We shall still get grumbles about the CBC; the Socreds will still believe that they are the only ones with a line to Divine Headquarters; wheat will — like Quebec — remain a problem. But in the East we'll put up with it, and in the West they'll have to. There aren't really any alternatives, now that Seattle is having riots, and Berkeley is under armed guard.

A SEPARATE STATE?
IT'S NOW POSSIBLE

Ernest Watkins

Ernest Watkins is a lawyer who lives in Calgary. He has written a number of articles and books.

What is it that turns a Western Canadian — some Western Canadians — into separatists? They are not oppressed — the Mounties are no rougher than the Quebec Provincial Police, if that. They have no language problems — if you want to speak French in Calgary, fine, but don't expect anyone to understand it. Their religions, save that of the Doukhobors, have been met with tolerance. Their real complaint is this: Western Canadians are neglected, ignored. They make up almost a quarter of the population of Canada and no one outside the Toronto and Montreal Stock Exchange bothers a damn about them. For most people in Ottawa, they feel, Canada ends somewhere between Sarnia and Thunder Bay and then miraculously reappears again at Yellowknife.

Western Canada produces grain, cattle and hogs and every kind of mineral in abundance, and all that has been accomplished by the people of Western Canada in well under a century, starting literally from scratch. Most of their production is exported and is immensely important to Canada's balance of trade. Yet what happens? The exports that Western Canadians themselves handle — beef and natural gas to the United States, coal and ore to Japan — flourish and expand. Those taken under the control of Ottawa wither on the vine. So there is a world surplus of wheat? If the marketing of Canada's grain was still in the hands of private enterprise in Winnipeg, they feel, we might have sold a lot more of it.

Take Canadian crude oil as another example. Production in Alberta is still restricted by government decree. Canadian wells could supply the whole of the country's needs easily if the pipelines were extended further east into Quebec, and the West would be very glad to do that at its own expense. But what happens? East of the Ottawa Valley the market is reserved for imported crude oil from the Caribbean and further east. And the reason? So that gasoline may be sold in Eastern Canada for a few cents less. You wouldn't want to ask the people of Quebec and the Maritimes to pay more than they need for gasoline and oil, would you? Yet when it comes to the farm machinery

Reprinted with permission of Ernest Watkins from *Saturday Night*, September 1970.

that Western Canada needs as much as Quebec needs oil, Ottawa has allowed the international manufacturers to gouge the Western Canadian farmer over the price of tractors like nobody's business. Who cares? The farmers haven't voted Liberal in years, and the two Canadian Prime Ministers who came from the West this century were dead losses anyway. Look after the Ontario manufacturer and your Party will never lack funds for an election campaign.

Finally, there are the Olympic Games. Everyone knows that Vancouver, at Garibaldi Park, has about the best site in the world for the winter Olympics and British Columbia stood a very good chance of winning the contest for the honour. But what happens? Montreal bounces in to make a bid for the Olympics themselves, puts up a hell of a song and dance in support, and bores its way into first place for the grand prize. Vancouver loses out, for you couldn't possibly have both Olympics in the same country in the same year. The Winter Olympics go to Denver, where the altitude will play havoc with the contestants, and the rest of Canada, including the West, will have to shoulder the $500 million or so bill that Mayor Drapeau will run up and be unable to pay. Where is the justice in that?

These are the kind of complaints of neglect that Western Canada has had for years. They are plausible, if not objectively true. Their real root lies in the fact that Western Canadians have never had enough votes or capital of their own to come anywhere near to calling the tune. In the West they are all newcomers — if a Western Canadian was not himself born somewhere else, the odds are his parents were — and very few of them indeed come with any working capital at all.

If they homesteaded, they borrowed from banks and insurance companies on mortgage and later watched those banks and insurance companies move smartly in to foreclose and sell when the Depression came. That is ancient history now, a legend, and like many legends still a present and bitter recollection for those it touched.

If the newcomer was interested in lumber or mining, he was bound to accept the position of hired man, as prospector, engineer or manager, or what have you, to win a start from those who would put up the capital that had to be risked. Were Eastern Canadians interested in supplying that kind of capital? They were not. The first commercial strike of oil, at Turner Valley, Alta., was financed through Calgary, but thereafter the costs of exploration rose to figures that only the international companies could meet. The next major discovery, at Redwater, Alta., was made by Imperial Oil, an American subsidiary. Since then Canadians have been able to benefit on the fringes of development, but they have never been able to achieve a dominant position.

This is a familiar tale. If it did make potential separatists of some Western Canadians, that separatism has so far been latent. The urges towards separatism have always been economic and if the economic objections to it were the stronger — as they were — the idea could never really get off the ground. There was nothing else to lift it.

What has changed in the last year or so has been the arrival of Japan. Japan has become a very attractive country to Western Canada in very short order. It is already a major market for the raw materials that Western Canada can produce in such abundance and Japan's remarkable growth and prosperity seem to guarantee that this market must expand. Japan is equally a source of capital for Canadian development to which no strings are attached. Japan does not want to bargain for rights to Canadian water when it negotiates to buy Canadian coal. And Japan is as good a source of supply as any in the world for the manufactured goods that Western Canada cannot make for itself. Japan is an ideal trading partner for Western Canada on the basis of strict trade alone. For the first time Western Canada can become a viable independent state, provided Japan is prepared to make a fully reciprocal treaty with it.

Were Canada to break up, the four Western Provinces, plus Ontario from Thunder Bay westwards and Yukon and the North West Territories, would coalesce as a unit, with British Columbia and Alberta leading and dominating the new state. It would at once become a Pacific Rim country and turn its back on the East. Premier Bennett of British Columbia might wish to take over Washington and Oregon to round off the domain (would it be his domain?) but this would be an attractive, not an essential, addition. Canada West would be a viable state, with a population approaching that of Australia. If it could avoid dreams of grandeur (and the cost of preparing for their realization) it could be a most prosperous country, and one whose political complexion would be unlikely to give the strategists in Washington, D.C. real cause for concern.

What part has Quebec played, positively or negatively, in moulding the thinking and sentiment of Western Canada? The answer given will depend very much on the age of the person giving it. The strongest disapproval of Quebec has always come from the remnants of the original Anglo-Saxon immigrants from Britain, and it has a simple base: Quebec is not loyal to the Crown, and that is that. Nothing will change this state of mind — it is that, not an argument — but since the present lifespan of most of those who think this way is short, politically it is a fact of diminishing importance.

In the West, disapproval of Quebec springs mainly from one source, the impression that Quebec is the spoilt child of the federation and claims special consideration because of her unhappy economic past. What other Province is able to turn so many federal-aid programmes into pure cash hand-outs?

Separatism in Western Canada, such as it is, is so far a negative thing, a reaction against, having nothing like the positive belief in Canada as a nation that the majority holds. The men and women who first peopled the West were there to build a wider, stronger and more prosperous Canada in the process of finding a new life for themselves, and in their own terms they have succeeded. They would be distressed and shaken if Canada ceased to be a part of the Queen's Realms, but they would not wish to break up Canada on that account. That would do nothing to restore their lost dream. And it should not be forgotten that the United States has long since drawn off many of those who were dissatisfied with Canada as a country.

As of now, Western Canada as a separate state is a neat and tidy intellectual plan and no one will die on the barricades fighting for its birth. That is the final test. Loyalty to something new can spring fully armed from the blood of martyrs. It will not be generated by cups of coffee served in a hundred discussion groups.

BRITISH COLUMBIA A HUNDRED YEARS AFTER CONFEDERATION

Leonard W. Meyers

Leonard Meyers is a Vancouver writer and cartoonist.

"It could only happen in British Columbia," a *cliché* perennially and somewhat smugly indulged in by the rest of Canada seems to have gained a measure of respectability in the year 1970. The December 9th civic election in Vancouver was a point in question. If ever a practical joke was perpetrated on the voters of Canada's third largest city, this was it. Frivolous would be an understatement.

With the mayor up for re-election, along with ten aldermen, nine school trustees, and seven parks board commissioners, Vancouver electors, when nomination day ended, were confronted with a staggering array of 105 candidates to choose from. Many of these — especially in the ranks of the independents — were triflers. At best, these mustered only a meagre five percent of the total vote.

Apart from Mayor Campbell, eleven other candidates vied for the city's top job.

Of these, only three could honestly have been considered serious contenders. They included the incumbent, Thomas Campbell, his chief opponent William C. Gibson, a University of British Columbia academic, and Tony Gargrave, a former provincial NDP MLA, who led his party to complete defeat in its first all-out partisan assault on city hall.

When the ballots were finally counted, after a long and tedious night of waiting, Mayor Tom Campbell of the NPA (Non-Partisan Association) along with six NPA incumbent aldermen were returned to council, thus maintaining the *status quo.*

Of the record 43 candidates running for aldermen the same three TEAM (The Electors' Action Movement), and one COPE (Committee of Progressive Electors) incumbent were also returned. The NDP failed to win a single seat. This, despite a near-record 45.5 percent turnout of eligible voters.

During the heat of the campaign controversial Mayor Campbell was subjected to a barrage of vilification and abuse second only to that traditionally reserved for Premier Bennett.

Suddenly law and order became a dirty word. Police protection — pardon us, "brutality" — a sick joke. And Campbell was characterized as

Reprinted with permission of *Canadian Commentator,* Volume 15, No. 2, February 1971.

the Spiro Agnew of Vancouver civic politics. He was equated, by one of his leading opponents, to Hitler and then again to the Jews because of his rigid stance against the Hippies, Yippies, rioters and lawless revolutionaries. He was further branded an opportunist, an exhibitionist, a second-class mayor, and a fascist. "Strangely enough," observed a puzzled citizen, "considering the similarity between fascism and communism, not one of his leftist detractors called him a communist."

He also became the favourite whipping-boy of the B.C. Civil Liberties Association, Vietnam Action Committee, the Vancouver Liberation Front, and other radical and leftist elements in the city.

At a U.B.C. campus rally he was even physically attacked by a non-student, self-styled Maoist who leaped on the stage and threw punches — and an ashtray — at the mayor before he was restrained. The attacker was later charged and sentenced to one month for assault.

Ridiculed for trying to garner the votes of the "sweet old ladies in tennis shoes" with his war-on-Hippies campaign, his enemies, after the election, must have concluded that Vancouver abounds with that kind of senior dolls.

Obviously the bulk of the citizens were satisfied with "Tom Terrific" (a derisive appellation conjured up by a Vancouver cartoonist, but one which backfired badly to the mayor's obvious advantage) and his record.

The fact remains, Vancouver has seen its greatest era of construction and development since he came on the scene. For example, high rise apartments were unknown in this city before he entered the civic scene and forced the issue. Today, Vancouver is a metropolitan city. A bit controversial and never dull, Campbell is really a maverick, as unconventional and colourful as the unrestrained, booming city he represents.

Apart from Yippies and triflers running for public office, not with any real chance of winning but rather to make a mockery of the democratic process, the most bizarre incident of the election was the entrance of a second "Tom" Campbell, real name Andrew Thomson, 20, into the mayoralty race. This was generally looked upon as an attempt to confuse the public and raid the senior Campbell's returns. To some extent it succeeded. An unknown warehouseman won almost five thousand votes, possibly most at the expense of the original Thomas J. Campbell.

If this was a personal victory for the mayor's namesake, it was short-lived. The following morning the police zeroed in on his South Vancouver home and arrested the fourth-placed mayoral aspirant charging him with drug trafficking and assault causing bodily harm. He was recognized as the wanted man from a campaign newspaper picture the day before the election.

As for the young Yippie mayoralty candidate, at least she was original. Campaigning on a platform of repealing the law of gravity "so everyone can get high," she managed to scrape up over 800 votes.

As we said, it could only happen in British Columbia. Struck by the ludicrous aspects of the election just past, the present city council is now considering tightening up election regulations to make it more difficult for last-minute pranksters to make a show running for public office.

On January 1st, 1971, British Columbia launched centennial celebrations commemorating its 100th anniversary of Confederation. It is hoped that the spirit of the occasion will help smooth some of the economic difficulties and labour problems which have beset the province in the past year.

Labour strife in 1970 was the unwelcome guest. It was rampant most of the year. It may again be the party-pooper in 1971.

The year was barely gone when some 1800 public transit workers, mainly bus drivers, in Vancouver and Victoria went on strike against B.C. Hydro, asking for more pay and improved working conditions. This strike is seen as the latest weapon with which Labour proposes to challenge the B.C. government's Mediation Commission (Bill 33 and compulsory arbitration), a quasi-judicial body completely ignored by the Amalgamated Transit Union in its bargaining with the B.C. Hydro and Power Commission.

So, last year's "confrontation", deferred when a government mediator was appointed, a move not now contemplated, could be here.

Referring to that near-encounter, outgoing president of the B.C. Federation of Labour, Al Staley, had this to say: "Such a confrontation could develop into a death struggle. It could topple the Socred government, or it could destroy the trade union movement as it is known today." The question uppermost in his mind, he went on to say, was whether labour could actually win such a struggle. And that is why the labour movement, when confrontation day appeared imminent last summer over the construction tie-up, pulled back from the brink.

And now from the toils of labour to the floodgates of the Skagit.

This latest controversy revolves around the intention of the Seattle City Power and Light Co. to raise the Ross Dam and flood the Skagit Valley some seven or eight miles north of the international boundary into British Columbia. Needless to say, indignant cries of anguish on the part of ecologists, conservationists, sportsmen and political oppositionists are raised almost daily denouncing the Bennett government's latest "'give-away." The present provincial government is being made the scapegoat. It ostensibly has perpetrated the latest sellout of our natural heritage to the dastardly Yanks for a "mess of pottage."

While most British Columbians deplore the further flooding of this scenic recreational valley some 100 miles south-east of Vancouver, the fact is that there is a case for flooding, to turn the area into a recreational lake-resort area complete with beaches, camping, boating, fishing, etc. Today it is an expanse of smelly mud flats. There is also the fact that the Social Credit government wasn't even in power when the initial agreements were concluded. In the provincial files in Victoria there is ample evidence about conclusive negotiations between Victoria and Seattle from as far back as four years before the Socreds assumed power. The scheme was approved by the International Joint Commission — a body set up specifically to deal with negotiations pertaining to international waters — in 1942.

In essence, what the Socred government did upon assuming power in 1952, was to finally ratify, in the late 'sixties, an already completed set of international negotiations concluded by its predecessors. These included a firm price for the further flooding of the valley and loss of wildlife. Before doing so, Lands and Forests Minister Ray Williston negotiated a new and better agreement than the original one. Yet it is for this that he is being condemned now. "It should never have been allowed," they say, and perhaps they are right. Recreational areas, especially within a few hours' drive from Vancouver, will be at a premium one day.

British Columbia may be 100 years old. But its chief advocate and architect for the past 19 years has just recently turned a spry and youthful 70. The man, Premier W. A. C. Bennett, is probably the only politician in Canada who not only thinks, but acts and appears to be getting younger as he racks up the years in office. Elected to the B.C. Legislature in 1942, and becoming premier in 1952, he seems to be good for another two election rounds barring any unforseen eventualities.

At a time when most men have retreated to the quiet backwaters of retirement, this durable politician seems to be endowed with perpetual vigour — to the chagrin of his political foes. And despite the maturity of the years, he can still look at today's youth through youthful eyes. "The problems," he maintains, "we're having with some of our children now is because the parents have been too soft with them. But over all, I would say that this younger generation is the best ever. They're better trained, better educated, and better thinkers . . . As for the generation gap, there's always been a generation gap. And it's good. A father should never try to be a brother to his son. He must be a father. There's a rivalry that's good for both of them . . . ."

For some of the grown-ups, especially politicians of another stripe, and their antics — anti-B.C. antics — he has harsher words. He feels strongly about the present federal government treating Quebec like a favoured child, and British Columbia like an unwanted one. He argues that Ottawa takes half a billion more out of British Columbia annually than it puts back, while it pours one billion more into Quebec yearly than the total taxes collected in that province. This to him is particularly iniquitous because British Columbia is one of North America's major growth areas.

Bennett thinks that Ottawa is completely run by three Quebeckers (Trudeau, Marchand and Pelletier), hence the senior government's pro-Quebec policies. As for being labelled anti-Quebec, he laughs: "Nonsense. We're the only province which ever lent Quebec one hundred million dollars on a handshake, and at a lower than market interest rate. . . ."

Will Mr. Bennett go on being premier forever? The answer obviously is, no. But one would never know it from the latest B.C. Social Credit League Convention in Vancouver. Once again the question of a successor to the premier was quietly shelved. The Socreds obviously do not want to get rid of him. Far from it. But the inevitable will have to be faced sooner or later — like the death of a loved one in the family. There certainly are aspirants for the leadership, Attorney-General Les Peterson, Minister of Municipal Affairs Dan Campbell, and Rehabilitation Minister P. A. Gaglardi, to mention a few. It's just that, well, no one really has the courage to declare himself openly as long as the beloved architect of the "good life" chooses, and remains equal, to the strenuous task of leadership.

THE WEST IS READY TO REVOLT

John Barr and Owen Anderson

Two influential Albertans state their case for separatism.

Perhaps only a westerner can understand the kind of helpless anger westerners have felt for the past decade or so as they have tried, and failed, to get a hearing for their unique regional perspective. On those rare occasions when the national media do discover that there is a part of Canada beyond Thunder Bay, Ontario, we are treated to quickie analyses, facile in thought and shallow in execution. Sometime in 1969, for instance, the media began to awaken to the existence of separatist movements in this area, none of which is presently too impressive in either intellectual terms or in numbers. (In this sense, the existing western separatist organizations resemble their counterparts in Quebec in the late Fifties and, like them, will probably be replaced in time by quite different and more formidable movements.) Most of the resulting analyses were journalistic crisis-pieces and tended to look for simple single causes at the root of the agitation for change. The commonest theory at the time, and probably the theory that has gained the widest acceptance in central and eastern Canada, is the simplistic notion that if the western wheat surplus could be sold, western bitching would probably fade away.

Now, obviously, there is some force to this "wheat politics" interpretation of the West: western frustration at the mediocre record of federal government grain agencies in penetrating world markets is a continuing source of irritation, especially in rural areas. But the sense of western injustice transcends rural-urban categories. A sense of persecution fills the hearts of many westerners who feel the grain pinch little or not at all.

Many westerners in all four provinces feel that their legitimate economic needs and aspirations are not being looked after by the federal authorities. Wheat is only one chapter in this story. Others include the failure of the federal government to bring about a deeper penetration of the U.S. market for western oil and natural gas. Another chapter is the use by the federal government of fiscal devices, such as the change in capital cost allowances for construction of office buildings, which have an uneven effect across the country and have worked their greatest hardship on western cities such as Vancouver, Edmonton and Calgary.

Perhaps the most important evi-

From *The Unfinished Revolt,* John Barr and Owen Anderson, eds. (Toronto: McClelland and Stewart Ltd.), 1971.

dence of economic callousness by the federal government toward the West was Edgar Benson's White Paper on taxation. Proposed changes in the Income Tax Act could have struck a serious, if not mortal, blow at mining and oil companies on which the western economy depends most precariously. The thought that Benson was prepared to sabotage U.S. investment in western Canada as part of a federal tax reform scenario outraged westerners, not because they love Americans but because they know what the alternative to American investment is for *them*: a return to economic stagnation. In the battle for tax reform, it seemed clear, Edgar Benson was prepared to fight to the last westerner.

In some ways, however, the federal government has injured our pride worse than our pocketbooks.

One example was the creation of Channel 11 in Edmonton. For many years educational television authorities in Alberta lobbied for a VHF educational TV station. This was possible in Edmonton, as in few other areas, because of its remoteness from American stations and a large open space on the VHF broadcast band. The upshot of this lobbying was an eventual decision by federal authorities to permit a temporary educational outlet broadcasting nine hours each weekday on a VHF band, operating in conjunction with a French-language outlet. It was announced that at the end of a three-year period the great generosity of the federal government in allowing this outlet would terminate, the entire station would become a French-language outlet for the full broadcasting day, and the educational TV would have to move to cablevision or UHF — although only a small minority of people have UHF receiving sets.

A small issue? Perhaps. But the creation of a French-language station in Edmonton — where fewer than 4% of the viewers list French as their mother tongue, but almost 8% list German and another 8% Ukrainian as their mother tongue — says some interesting things about the determination of the federal government to push a bilingual policy on all parts of the country, regardless of local needs or circumstances. It also says some interesting things about who is influential within the country and who is not.

The list of minor irritations of this kind could be adumbrated at some length. But let us press on to the largest irritant: the stereotype of the West propagated in the media of this country. We all know what this stereotype involves. Westerners do not really object to being portrayed as the Cousin Clems of Confederation. But in an age when liberal scribes in Toronto and Montreal would leap in outrage at a derogatory generalization about a race or creed, it is puzzling to find them helping to perpetuate an insulting stereotype of the average westerner that blends equal parts of cloddiness, parochialism and, most important, anti-French bigotry.

There is unfortunately a small core of pure anti-French prejudice in parts of the West, particularly in some rural areas and among the less educated. This prejudice usually exists in an inverse relationship to the amount of actual contact these persons have had with French-speaking people. It is rooted in ignorance and fear of people who are different. There is this kind of prejudice in the West, but there is no evidence that it is any more widespread here than in other parts of Canada.

The *major* opposition to the pro-

French movement of national policy over the past decade came from westerners who had nothing in particular against the French: they simply resented Ottawa imposing on their style of life and habits when Pierre Trudeau suggested that a substantial minority of people outside the Ontario border should have special language facilities, special schools and special language rights not available to other ethnic groups that were at least as numerically important in their communities as the French, if not more important. The contention that bigotry is an exclusive western product is itself a form of bigotry against the West.

And so, if some westerners are bitter about their treatment by the rest of this country, they have understandable reasons for their bitterness. But it is, in the final analysis, in the political arena that the roots of the present discontent lie.

Consider the current frustration of politically conscious westerners faced with the dearth of real political choices in the current federal scene. On one side we have Pierre Trudeau: a man with an obvious design for Canada in his head but also, regrettably, a man who seems incapable of being *simpatico* with westerners, a man chained to his somewhat parochial Montreal bourgeois past.

And then there is Robert Stanfield: a man of fine, quiet, decent qualities, but obviously not a modern politician and certainly not a man sufficiently sensitive to western vibrations to realize something is drastically out of whack in our federal system.

Réal Caouette is an interesting regional figure, unfortunately too tied to a peculiarly Quebec protest movement. And the New Democratic Party is currently riding a wave of nationalist hysteria that has quite blinded it to the growing regionalization of the country.

This lack of real and viable political choices is a factor that deepens the discontent of westerners. For us, there do not seem to be very many channels left for legitimate political change at the national level. And the feeling of bitter helplessness is underlined by the growing power of economic nationalism in our politics.

The average westerner is not inclined to accept all the arguments of the economic nationalist at face value, because he knows from hard experience that too often in our history economic nationalism has been used by eastern interests to maintain their control over the rest of the country. He knows that the West developed an economy heavily dependent upon foreign capital and vulnerable to fluctuations in its movement. To start meddling with this movement without exercising the greatest possible care and consultation could spell economic disaster for western Canadians.

But simply listing our complaints against central Canada is not enough. Conscientious westerners must try to make this country work — in a more just fashion. If, however, it becomes obvious that Canada is not a viable proposition politically, or if the present injustice deepens, there is no very persuasive moral argument for the West trying to integrate itself into a burning building.

Therefore:

1. We must strive for a more justly constituted Canada.

2. If Canada loses her political viability, the West must strike out against the odds to try and build an independent state in this corner of North America.

How would a more just Canada be constituted? By reducing the power of the central government to dictate arbitrarily to the regions or provinces.

First, there would be some form of institutional safeguard for regional prerogatives: perhaps a reformed senior chamber for the House of Commons composed of an equal number of elected representatives from each region of the country to counterbalance representation by population.

Second, there would be a nationwide guaranteed-income plan, financed by the federal government, to replace the present ineffective patchwork of regional incentives and regional development programs. The plan would create a modest guaranteed income, sufficient to enable one to live at a spartan but healthy level.

Beyond that, the problem of regional inequality would be left to the working of the free market and stepped-up programs of manpower retraining and mobility grants by the federal government.

Third, there would be a reformed judiciary with provision for regional nominations. Such a judiciary would be more capable of intepreting the jurisdiction of the federal and provincial authorities fairly and credibly.

Last, there would be a modification in the distribution of constitutional powers to prevent an excessive accumulation of power by the federal government. The central clause in a revised constitution would limit the spending by the federal government to a certain percentage of the gross national product. This would restrain any temptation to move into too many areas and, more importantly, compel the federal authorities to reexamine their spending priorities periodically in the light of available funds. It would also ease the growing pressure on the provincial authorities, who are saddled with some of the most expensive government responsibilities — particularly education and

health — but who have too little access to direct taxation. The present "peace, order and good government" clause of the BNA Act, which assigns all residual powers to the federal government, would finally, be replaced with a clause designating all residual powers to the regions or provinces.

Let us assume that our drive for a more justly constituted Canada is thwarted, or that Canada begins to disintegrate politically, beginning with Quebec. What then?

The question of an independent West would have to be squarely confronted.

Would a thinly spread-out, thousand-mile-wide entity with fewer than six million people be politically viable on the same continent as the United States? (The answer is less obvious than it may first seem. Such a nation would lack credibility — but then so does Canada, and so does Israel. Severance from Canada might, by the very act of reducing western numbers, heighten the region's "siege consciousness," and thus our unity and determination to survive. It is this siege consciousness — this sense of being surrounded by more than 200 million aliens — that has made it possible for Quebec to retain so much of her identity. Whether, in the long run, *any* effective resistance to continentalism is possible by either Quebec or the West is a moot point).

Would the four western provinces unite, placing their hopes on their shared history, or would British Columbia elect to go it alone? Should we talk about a common market relationship with Ontario, or would we be better advised to proceed entirely by ourselves?

Political questions aside, could the economic base in the four western provinces sustain independence? These questions cannot yet be answered. Put so baldly, they sound somewhat bizarre. And of course they are . . . for the moment. They are not serious questions yet. But we live in very fluid times. Two days before the act of kidnapping James Cross, who would have anticipated the upsurge of FLQ terrorism, with its incalculable consequences for Canada? We face the haunting fear that this nation may rupture more suddenly than anyone now thinks possible, forcing us to ask these questions and answer them with unseemly haste. Surely it makes sense to begin turning them over in our minds now, while we still have time to make sense of them.

J.B.

A great sense of powerlessness pervades western Canadian history, although the West has generated provincial leaders who have fought for provincial interests. But where were the federal leaders who should have given expression to the frustrations of a political process that is essentially manipulative? Where were the leaders to protest the exploitation of those regions with insufficient federal representation? Western Canada's federal representatives are essentially spineless, ever ready to mouth the party line and enjoy the political fruits that accrue from party subservience.

The West has found itself with a weak and ineffective voice in an essentially colonial-style governing system. Even if the West returned to Ottawa a member of the governing party from every constituency it could not, in the final analysis, exert any appreciable influence. And so the West is a colony, albeit in a very sophisticated and 20th-century sense.

The West does not know itself. It is not researched. It is largely unknown to its own people — sociologically culturally, economically and especially politically.

Leaders in the West, with certain obvious exceptions, have been timid and often passive in dealings with the federal governments. In many cases, they have simply been outfoxed, outnegotiated by their federal counterparts. Until recently, the problem has been two-fold: external manipulation and internal incompetence.

Then too, western provinces, particularly Alberta and British Columbia, are dismissed by federal officials as so-called "have" provinces (the basis of which is an arbitrary and misleading equalization formula that distorts the great disparities within a province) which thus do not need special consideration or concessions. But there are many western Canadians, particularly Indians and Métis, living in poverty, who earn far less than they require for a decent standard of living. The "average" figures only hide this reality.

Then, what about cultural poverty? What about the people who will be alienated from society because of a lack of educational opportunities? What are we doing to prepare and plan for the vast changes we know will take place in the next two or three decades?

Despite this cultural and psychological repression, we are witnessing a renewed interest and revival in the rights of western Canada. It is a renewal, with intellectual overtones, of that commitment which has alternately surfaced and submerged but has always been a vital factor in western Canadian history. The western farmers are experiencing agricultural adversities and again see themselves — as they did in the days after World War I — as the playthings of the high-tariff manipulators. They see markets cut off and prices reduced to levels that make it hardly worthwhile producing at all. They see the federal government discriminate against the West in its selective depreciation and in the White Paper tax proposals. More and more the people are becoming socially perplexed, frustrated and angry. They desire to preserve, foster and encourage the quality of life in western Canada, an intangible cultural psychology which makes the West just as different from the rest of Canada as the French language and French civil law make Quebec different.

Before industrial technology and urbanization freed western Canadians from a real engagement with nature, the influence of the land, the hardships, and perhaps the myth of the West contributed most to the distinctive community that is western Canada. The land held, and still does hold, a challenge and a charm. Difficult to define, but omnipresent, its incomparable vistas and rugged inhospitality called forth a response from western Canadians, who found a real source of identification, a feeling for its spaciousness and its grandeur and the psychological effect of these combined geographic factors.

It was the myth of the land, the "Go west, young man" tradition that engendered and nourished the exuberance and vitality that is synonymous with western Canada and has played such a vital part in its development. The land and the harsh climate have had a purifying effect not only on its native-born, but on those who came to savor its quality and stayed to nourish a cooperative community that visitors recognize and admire but cannot define and emulate.

The great shift of population from the distinctive western rural lands to new and growing cities is even now producing a new urban identity. But, while the land still exerts its influence on western Canadian culture, it is increasingly becoming the man-made environment that is the formulative influence on the western social character. It is precisely this that should be the concern of western politicians and governments.

The West is not a carbon copy of any other region in Canada or the U.S., despite wholehearted attempts to make our cities just that. The West is not a carbon copy of the East, nor is it an extension of American society.

The West wants to preserve its independence, to create opportunities for involvement and fulfillment, to develop its own social and cultural institutions and to give expression to its distinctiveness.

It is a distinctiveness that is worth preserving, that makes the West in its own particular way just as different and just as much entitled to special status as any other province or region in Canada. The federal government's perversion of the federative principle is doing much to perpetuate the alienation of the West. The West wants the right to develop freely, creatively and in its own style. To secure this right the West has been, and will be, prepared to revolt.   O.A.

GEORGE BOXALL IS GOING BROKE ON THE RICHEST LAND IN THE WORLD

James Quig

James Quig is a frequent contributor to Weekend Magazine.

You can see George Boxall's spread long before you get to it; Edgeley, Sask., isn't much of a place on the map but even little towns stand tall on the prairie horizon and George lives right next door to the grain elevator.

It isn't a fancy place. When they talk about Western farmers wintering down South or burning up the crap tables in Vegas they aren't talking about George. The Boxalls winter in Edgeley. George runs the bridge club all winter on a $34 budget and says it's plenty. Everybody brings a mickey and there's always a nice lunch.

George owns one of the 85,000 farms in Saskatchewan. He cultivates about 500 acres of grain and runs about 35 head of beef cattle. He was born on the plains 52 years ago on the farm his father homesteaded in 1887. He loves the way he lives. He figures he can produce enough food in a year to feed 200 people and he's proud of that. He works hard and gets his hands dirty but it's clean dirt,

he says, and anyway, hard work never killed a man.

Monica, his wife, is from Manchester and had never even heard of Saskatchewan until she met George in England during the war. But she was young and plucky and together they built their home 30 miles east of Regina. It wasn't easy for her at first. George says it took them three years before they were able to catch up with the bills down at the store. And it was so different from Manchester — so vast and desolate and cold in the winter. But the people were all so nice even though she didn't know a thing about farming and she just seemed to fit right in. She still misses the availability of libraries and theatres and they still don't have running water in the house and a car would be nice and . . . but you can't have everything.

And the boys are doing so well. David, 23, off discovering Australia; Richard, 22, graduating this Christmas with a degree in education and Michael, 17, wanting to be a lawyer.

There is only one thing wrong with it all. The Boxalls are slowly but surely going broke because George

47

can't sell his grain.

"Going broke with my bins full of wheat," he says. "And it's not a good feeling."

Here's why:

Canada isn't the only exporter of wheat in the world. She isn't even the world's biggest wheat grower. The Soviet Union, one of our best wheat customers, grows vastly more than we do. And, like Canada, almost all of the wheat-exporting countries have had bumper crops in recent years. As a result the market has dwindled drastically and the exporting countries have more than they can sell.

So George Boxall's bins runneth over. He can't sell as much so he can't *buy* as much. And that's why so many Regina stores are running Going Out Of Business sales and you keep hearing stories about prairie depression: When wheat doesn't move in Saskatchewan nothing moves.

We were out in the barn where George was feeding a motherless Aberdeen Angus calf from a bottle.

"Can't stand working a tractor," he says, "although most farmers love that part of it. I like the animals. I guess I wouldn't have stuck it out this long had I not had the animals. That's where the security is today. Animals. Wheat's too big a gamble."

Still, he talked very lovingly about the bumper crop he took off 250 acres of land last year.

"Six thousand bushels from land that usually produces 3,000. You sure get a good feeling when you produce a crop like that."

It didn't do him much good: He produced $7,500 worth of wheat but was only able to sell 2,400 bushels — approximately $3,000 worth. The rest of it is stored in barns and sheds all over his property.

The calf gulped the last of the formula and George announced he was now going to water the bull.

"I'll have to close the barn door," he said.

"How come?"

"I let him out of the pen to drink. Don't worry, he won't hurt you — if you stand well back."

We stood well back.

"You can't turn your back on them, though," George warned.

He needn't have bothered. The bull wasn't thirsty and, happily, was soon ushered back into the bullpen.

"I figure I can last another five years under the existing conditions," he said as we drove down the dusty road to the quarter-section (160 acres) he was working. "After that I'll be down and out. Five years in the army and 24 on the farm and it could all go down the drain in five years. Some will fall before me, some after. The older farmers are OK. The established farms that are all paid for, they'll pull through. It's the younger ones I feel sorry for. The ones who expanded when we were making those big sales to China and things looked so rosy. The ones who piled up big debts then are the ones in trouble today.

"I'm luckier than some. I'm used to being hard up. But some of them spent money like water. Real big-time spenders some of them. Of course there's nothing like a farmer for spending. But I should talk. I went out and bought another quarter-section myself in 1967.

"I don't owe a lot — $6,000. And I could have paid that all off had we been able to sell that big crop last year. Still, we don't have the flush toilets or running water . . ."

He estimated he would take about 60 acres of his best land out of production this year, deliberately reducing his yield.

"I can only think of one thing that hurt me more than that," he said.

"What's that?"

"When I joined the Canadian Army and I couldn't put down that I was a Canadian citizen."

"Why not?"

"You had to put down British origin — and that really hurt. I was very, very insulted by that."

On the way back to the house we stopped off at one of the sheds where he has stored some of last year's bumper crop. The wheat was spilling out of the cracks of the old building.

"Sad, eh," he said, running his hands through the grain. "You'd think we could find a way to get it to the people who need it — even if we had to give it away. My sister isn't planting at all this year at her place. She has 25,000 bushels on hand."

Back at the house, Monica served lunch, explaining that by raising their own beef, baking her own bread and growing a lot of the vegetables she is able to keep the food bill down to $60 a month. But that includes all of her cleaning materials.

"You know if I could sell just three-quarters of what I produce I wouldn't have a worry in the world," George said.

But things are bad all over the agricultural world, the Canadian Federation of Agriculture said in a report to the federal cabinet last April.

"Farming," it stated, "continues to be a seriously depressed industry. Scores of thousands of farm families have incomes which would be well below the poverty line on any acceptable definition. Take the example of the 430,000 farmers in the 1966 census. Approximately one-third had annual sales of $2,500 or less."

Incomes have sharply deteriorated in the last two years.

"Canadian farmers produce in a high-cost domestic economy and sell in a highly-protected, highly-subsidized, highly-organized international trade community.

"Lack of effective bargaining power, both as sellers of products and buyers of supplies needed in operations, add further to farmers' difficulties.

"Also, many farms are simply unable to put together the required capital, management and expertise to be viable economic units by today's standards."

The federation sees little room for optimism.

"Wheat faces a tough international market. The Canadian dairy industry is working on a national plan to equate supply with domestic demand in light of the world oversupply situation in which prices are at very low levels. Poultry and turkey meats are constantly under market pressure . . . and Canadian egg producers have an urgent need to tailor supplies to demand."

One bright note: "There does appear to be a possibility for market expansion in red meats, in feed grains and in oilseeds."

And that's why George is raising beef cattle: They pay the bills, bringing him in some $2,000 a year.

George started out in 1947 with a new tractor and 300 acres of land purchased at $20 an acre through the Veterans Land Act.

"It was pretty rough land," he says. "Full of rocks and gopher holes."

Disaster came early. In 1948 he was hit with the first of four short crops that he has faced in 23 years.

"We missed the rains and only got seven bushels to the acre. Just bad luck. A friend of mine two miles north got 25 bushels per acre the same year."

But they made out. He had a couple of cows and peddled milk to some of his neighbors at 10 cents a quart.

"I sold between 10 and 15 quarts a day and my gross income that year amounted to about $500."

In 1949 he decided that grain was too risky and went into the dairy business, starting off with four pure-bred Holsteins bought on time from a neighbor at $165 per cow.

But he was back into the grain business again by 1963.

"There was no choice. To keep going in the milk business I would have had to spend $25,000 on new equipment — and I just couldn't see it."

He sold the cows but started raising beef cattle — just in case the bottom ever fell out of the grain business.

* * *

Saturday night with the Boxalls. Michael says none of the young people are going into farming. A lot of the people he knows are moving right out of the province, many of them heading for Alberta and then out to British Columbia.

"The average age around here is at least 55," says George. "Some of them are getting pretty cranky about the situation."

"We have to find a way to get our wheat to the people who need it," says Michael. "Even if we have to advance them more credit."

His father says one of the problems is that Canada forgot about the little guys — the smaller customers like Peru and Brazil and the United Arab Republic — "when we were making all those big sales to Russia and China."

He says the last land sale around Edgeley was in 1967 at $137 an acre.

"You might get $60 for it now — if you could find a buyer. But who would want it when you can't sell the product?"

Another of the problems, says Michael, is that there isn't enough co-operation in Canada.

"The East doesn't care about the West and vice-versa. We're tied together by economics only."

His father agrees. "There should be more understanding in Canada. The spud farmer's problem in Prince Edward Island should be my problem, too."

Those Canadians living in the urban, industrialized areas of the country cannot afford to ignore the problems of the wheat farmer either. When he is in trouble, we all suffer in one way or another.

George says there should be more interchanging of students in Canada. Without it, in a land so vast, we will never breach the gap of understanding that exists between East and West.

"More kids should be able to come out here for the summer and live with westerners and we would send ours East. The schools should do more of that. And it should be available for many kids, not only the ones with the highest marks."

Monica serves a wonderful lunch and George explains that they don't get to town very often. Not even Regina, which is only 30 miles away.

"We have a garage and co-op store in Edgeley and I prefer to buy locally — even if I do have to pay a little more. If we didn't support them they'd go out of business and then where would we be?"

It was time to go and we all said goodbye. Outside, under a black prairie sky, George Boxall confided that one of his biggest worries right now was his tractor. It needed about

$600 worth of repairs. To pay for it he would have to dip into his savings — and he didn't like to do that because the prospects of ever putting it back in the bank looked rather gloomy.

"There won't be any farmers on this land after I'm done here," he said. "Sad, eh?"

We listened to the crickets for a few moments and wondered if tomorrow would be as hot.

"But don't make me out to be a crybaby. This is the land of plenty. It'll come back. It did in 1954 and it did in the 30s. It'll do it again. Farmers are optimists, you know. They have to be. We always say this is *next-year country.*"

"How's that?"

"Next year things are going to get better."

SASKATCHEWAN: THE GREAT DEPRESSION: 1970

Al Finkel

Al Finkel is Assistant Editor of Canadian Dimension.

Hodgeville is a small rural community in south-western Saskatchewan. A few years ago it was a town of about 300 people. It had a hospital, a hotel, several cafes and dozens of small shops. Most of the town's business came from the surrounding farms. It still does. But there's little business left. Nobody stays in the hotel; only one cafe is left in town; every second commercial establishment of five years ago is boarded up; the hospital has been closed. No one in Hodgeville will really be surprised if five years from now the name of their village is just a memory.

It is Saskatchewan's misfortune to be replete with dying Hodgevilles. It is Saskatchewan's further misfortune that the economic forces destroying the Hodgevilles are similar to the forces that will decide the future of the province as a whole. Saskatchewan, it might be said, is a big version of Hodgeville. For every little shop employing five people that a Hodgeville has closed, a Regina or Saskatoon company may have hired one more person to handle the new business. Economics of scale which result in a shifting of markets from the villages and hamlets to the cities also dictate a centralization of secondary industry operations in the cities in the East, Alberta and the U.S. Meanwhile, the small farmers, like the small communities, are being cast aside as "uneconomical." In an age of bigness, Saskatchewan is composed of small farms, small communities and small cities. And, unfortunately for Saskatchewan, of leaders of small vision.

Saskatchewan's politicians and businessmen are fond of speaking about Western "alienation." The West needs a "voice in Ottawa." According to this theory, the federal government is a captive of Quebec.

And if the lack of a Western *deus ex machina* doesn't totally explain why the Saskatchewan economy is in ruins, Premier Ross Thatcher has one more answer: "greedy union bosses." People are frightened, and populists like Thatcher are offering straw villains. One can only speculate what the populists would be saying if Saskatchewan had a sizable Jewish or black population.

Before judging Thatcher and company, one must understand the role they are playing: that of the Saskatchewan executive committee for government-subsidized private enterprise. Thatcher, in the preface to both his 1965 and 1966 budget speeches, said, "Help and assistance to private enterprise is the most effective way to open up and develop our province." But, for whom is the province being developed and at whose expense? Increasingly, workers and farmers are wondering if the invisible hand which turns private investment into public benefit hasn't been replaced by a visible hand turning public investment into private benefit.

Jerry Hudson, a member of Moose Jaw's labor council, outlined in an interview the recent performance of private enterprise in his city. Moose Jaw with a population of 42,000 has felt the effects of farmers' empty pockets as has every city and town in the province. But, according to the Thatcher dictum, the blow should have been cushioned by Moose Jaw's past luck in having secured private enterprise. Just the opposite has been the case, as business after business closes down. Private firms in Moose Jaw are not responsible to the people of the city; they are responsible to their owners, whose interests, contrary to the "invisible hand" theory, are not the same as those of the citizens of Moose Jaw.

The results: Robin Hood Mills, a subsidiary of International Milling (U.S.A.), which has been in Moose Jaw "as far back as the city has existed," has closed.

Gulf Oil has closed down its refinery. Of the 150 employed there, they have kept about 30 in asphalt, laid off the rest and centralized operations in Edmonton.

Prairie Bag Plant, a subsidiary of Bemis (U.S.A.), which employed 25 persons, has also left.

The big Canadian Pacific Railway repair depot in Moose Jaw has been closed down and centered in Winnipeg. Branch lines of the C.P.R. have in fact been closed all across the province.

Many of the workers who have lost their jobs as a result of these closures — especially the oil workers — were among the highest paid workers in the city. Many had started new homes just before the closures were announced.

"Now all we're getting is little outfits that pay the minimum wage," says Mr. Hudson.

The combined effect of major industries leaving and cashless farmers not buying has crippled service industries. "I know electricians and plumbers who haven't worked since Christmas. These people aren't even officially unemployed."

Moose Jaw Sash and Door has laid off 17 of its 25 employees. One plumbing firm which employed nine men "has laid off every guy and the owner is now working from his home. An electrical shop, which employed eight, is down to three."

All in all, Moose Jaw would seem a poor advertisement for the private enterprise way of doing things. Thatcher's argument is that Moose Jaw's city councillors and MLAs (Moose Jaw is New Democratic Party territory) have a negative view of free enterprise. Moose Jaw's Economic Development Board sponsored a seminar. A hired consultant did a study on Moose Jaw's specific problems. His analysis was that people weren't smiling enough. "If they'd smile, the directors in Pittsburg, New York, etc., would come in," mimicked Mr. Hudson.

The city's librarian takes the "smile and the multi-national corporations smile with you" argument seriously. Some high school kids were going to do a film: "Moose Jaw — the Dying City." The librarian wouldn't let them in for information.

One Moose Jaw alderman says "the city has to give tax incentives to compete with Winnipeg." But Moose Jaw would not be able to compete with Winnipeg or Edmonton even if its people went on a pilgrimage to New York City to beg . . . smiling all the while of course . . . private companies to locate in their city. Moose Jaw is a minor market far from major markets. While maximization of profits is the motive for locating or relocating industry, Moose Jaw always loses.

Bill Gilbey, president of the Saskatchewan Federation of Labour, says Moose Jaw is an extreme example of what is happening to the entire Sas-

katchewan economy. Decisions made by the large corporations and by a federal and provincial government dedicated to giving the vested interests "help and assistance" are insuring that Saskatchewan remains underdeveloped. The population and income statistics provide a depressing picture. The net value of farm incomes, according to provincial government figures, plummeted 46% in 1970. Considering that the 1969 figure was itself 27% below the 1967 figure, the net effect on a farm-dominated economy can well be appreciated. From April 1969 to April 1970 the province's population dropped by 18,000 to 943,000, a figure identical with the population count in mid-1964, the year Thatcher took power. As a result, official unemployment figures generally show only about five percent of the Saskatchewan work force as unemployed. But, as Mr. Gilbey points out, there is a great deal of "hidden unemployment" even apart from the population exodus.

Younger people who have worked two, three or four years in the labor force, pack up and go back to the farm and don't bother registering. Several thousand have headed back to the farm, although there is no work for them and they provide a further drain on the limited income of the farm family.

Further, there are large numbers of skilled tradesmen who, like the electricians and plumbers in Moose Jaw, are unable to find work for several months in a row. Few of these people are registered as unemployed. Then along comes the federal government with its "anti-inflation" program. At a time when Saskatchewan could not afford it, programs with federal government participation were held back. Meanwhile the provincial government, anxious that taxes on corporations and high incomes remain at a low level, showed little eagerness to take advantage of what little federal money was available.

The present recession has merely worsened what was already a very serious situation. The rationalization that is taking place everywhere in industry is hurting Saskatchewan greatly. Every city in the province has been affected by this tendency; Moose Jaw, as mentioned, the most. The companies, usually American, that have subsidiaries in the province are closing down or curtailing operations.

Codville in Prince Albert employed 27. One and a half years ago the manager walked in and said, "Everybody's finished." Goodyear closed its Regina operations and centered in Saskatoon. They had 20 Regina employees. A third were transferred; the rest were let go . . . Ackland's bought out Ashdown's, laying off 50 of the 80 employees . . . McGavin's Bakery curtailed operations in Saskatoon and shut down in Yorkton, leaving 20 jobless . . . Packing house plants have been closing down in the past five or six years in Saskatchewan. Burns in Prince Albert, a large plant in Prince Albert terms, and Inter-Continental in Saskatoon have both curtailed operations. They now do only certain processes here, and they have shrunk their staff. The examples are endless. Meanwhile the Hodgevilles lose their hardware stores and groceries, and the larger companies in Regina and Saskatoon gain a little. But the smaller shops in the two biggest cities are unable to compete.

Says Mr. Gilbey: "11th Avenue looks like it did in the Depression. For three or four blocks there's nothing but empty stores, most of them closed down during the last year." Two furniture companies had closed, and several clothing stores during 1970. Christy Grant's, a low-cost clothing outfit, employing six people, was among those forced to close. Christy Grant's has been a part of Regina for fifty years. Along one block on 11th the only two buildings without "vacant" or "clearing out" signs are the headquarters of the Liberal Party and the Social Credit Party. The NDP office on Quebec Street also stands among vacant shops.

Although big business and its Liberal Party work hard — and often successfully to divide farmers from workers, the farmers are threatened by a rationalization in agriculture that parallels that in industry. In the case of farms, what's happening is best described by the phrase "private collectivization." The myth of the family farm as the last bastion of small entrepreneurship is belied by the statistics of the Saskatchewan Economic Review on the number and size of farms. Increasingly only the larger farms which make extensive use of machinery are able to withstand the machinations of the farm-based industries and the cash shortages that result in bad crop years. Between 1961 and 1966, for example, despite a drop in the total number of farms, there was an increase from 1002 to 1276 farms of 2900 acres and over. But the number of farms of 600 acres or less dropped from 48,422 to 39,637. The task force on agriculture says 44% of rural Canada lives in poverty. Given the poverty of the farmers during the best of years (and 1961-1966 were comparatively good years) and the fact that small farms tended to be eliminated even in the good years, it is not hard to guess the fate of the Saskatchewan farmer now that the years of the huge grain sales to Communist countries have passed. The federal government's task force on agriculture proposed the speeding up of the private collectivization process. Greater efficiency and bigger profits for agri-business would be achieved by combining smaller private farms into larger private units.

Frank McCloy, regional co-ordinator of the Saskatchewan region of the National Farmers' Union, believes farmers are "more than ever" becoming disillusioned with traditional politics and economics. "Traditionally the farmer is production-oriented. He's a free enterpriser, believing that if he works hard, he'll survive . . . But as the corporations move in, he's seeing it's not so. Also the farmer sees that with constant inflation, he's being hurt the most."

Nevertheless, many farmers are seeking simple answers — sometimes the organized labor scapegoat of Thatcher and company, sometimes the deus ex machina to set Ottawa straight. One group appealing to the farmers for support using the latter device is the Palliser Wheat Growers' Association formed in April.

"We have every indication from people in government and the grain trade that if we represent the wheat farmer, we can obtain representation on the wheat board," writes organization president Walter Nelson, a John Deere implement dealer in Avonlea. But what would Mr. Nelson tell Ottawa if he were the "voice" of the farmer? Would he suggest that the government go into the farm machinery business so that the farmer would no longer be the victim of the farm machinery cartel's price fixing (as revealed in the Barber Commission report)?

Will Bob Ferguson, the managing director of the PWGA, formerly with Searle Grain, take on agri-business? The words of praise the PWGA has received from bankers, Conservative MPs and agri-business indicate which side it is on. Perhaps a hopeful sign is that at a packed June meeting of the association in Rosetown, the farmers reacted with unconcealed hostility to the arguments presented by the PWGA leadership.

Another sign is that Don Mitchell, the left-wing (Waffle group) candidate for the Saskatchewan NDP leadership at its July convention received significant farm support.

The Waffle group successfully put forward an agricultural resolution calling for public land assembly although its call for public ownership of farm-based industries was rejected in favor of "rationalization" of these industries (whatever that means in this case being left deliberately obscure).

Joe Roberts, head of Regina campus' political science department, points to the long range costs to the society of these capitalist collectivizations — the bill in welfare costs and municipal deterioration. "Are more huge ghettoized cities what we have to accept because it's profitable for agri-business to drive everybody off farms and into the cities?"

Prof. Roberts said that policies such as land assembly and public control of agri-business would make it possible to stop the erosion of farms and farm communities. He suggested other alternatives.

"Put it at the disposal of a region — given the technology available, markets, community needs, population, other forms of income production in that region, the people of the region can decide themselves what size farms are desirable and how many people will be directly engaged in farming there . . . Public collectivization and socialist planning are the only answers to private collectivization and capitalist planning."

Prof. Robert says that socialist planning is also the only hope for a diversified Saskatchewan economy. Private industry may have decided that Saskatchewan is a resource base, but the public doesn't have to accept this.

"This economy is an extractive economy. This is being expanded, not reduced. There's no significant secondary industry in Saskatchewan. We have a pulp mill (Parsons and Whittemore in Prince Albert), but we're not producing finished paper that we can market. We're rich in potash, but we have no real chemical fertilizer industry here. We have oil, but some of our oil refineries are being closed down."

The potash industries in Prince Albert and the pulp mill have been key achievements in Thatcher's "Help and assistance to private enterprise" program. The pattern can be simply described: public funds for infrastructure and capital costs, and private profits for foreign-owned corporations. There is planning but of the type that will suit the corporation's needs. A facade of public involvement is created, but when the real decisions are made, the communities involved are not consulted. In the Esterhazy area, for example, where International Minerals and Chemicals has its mine, "the whole business of industrial development is a hoax perpetrated on the residents of the area," according to Frank McCloy. The major costs for industrial development were borne by the communities involved.

"The provincial government undertook the cost of planning and offered cost sharing programs for roads, streets, sewer and water, etc. These were really not any different than what is available to other communities . . Any community that offered

objections to the limited assistance could then be given a choice — if you don't like the program, it is not forced upon you. Your town will die and some other centre will prosper instead. What responsible council could refuse to participate in the prosperity accruing from industrial development?" The land assessment in the rural municipalities of Langenberg and Spy Hill have tripled, but the mill rate the farmers pay still keeps going up . . . roads, snow removal, etc., must be supplied for the industry. Esterhazy has achieved the distinction of having the highest per capita debt of any municipality in Saskatchewan. The town's population has rocketed from 700 or 800 to 3600. And the new industry brought with it an "enormous amount of new construction" — some of which was chain stores whose operation broke the backs of small local businessmen (who, of course, were the mine's earliest supporters).

This year, however, there has been a huge cutback in potash production at IMC, eliminating almost 300 jobs in Esterhazy and the rural municipalities. They couldn't keep up with IMC while it was expanding; now they have to service it and pay increased welfare costs as well.

Why was production suddenly cut back 60%? Ross Thatcher announced a production limit last November, but the decision was hardly Thatcher's. The chief potash mining companies in Saskatchewan also have operations in New Mexico, operations which are not as efficient as the Saskatchewan mines. To avoid bankrupting their New Mexican operations, the companies asked Thatcher for "help and assistance to private enterprise." So Ross, the rugged individualist, set up the Potash Conservation Board to replace competition with cooperation among the potash mines.

Neither the potash mines nor the pulp mill have created the 80,000 jobs Thatcher promised to create during the 1964 campaign. The Prince Albert pulp mill, for example, created only 300 jobs despite Thatcher's promise of 1500. At what cost it is difficult to estimate. Yet despite the fact that government funds, partially equity capital, though mainly low-interest loans and low-cost services, built the mill, Thatcher accepts the priorities of the private U.S. company which he aided, Parsons and Whittemore. One of these is low wages. Recently the Prince Albert employees ended a strike and signed a contract under threat of compulsory arbitration. Thatcher said a low wage settlement was necessary since the company had said it would not build a second mill at Meadow Lake if the union's demands were met. Thatcher's reasoning: "We're just not going to let a bunch of union fellows — many of whom were on social aid a few years ago — say whether or not we'll get a pulp mill." In other words, asking for decent wages is equivalent to keeping out new industry. Undoubtedly, if one accepts the interests of the large monopolies as the interests of the people, this is true. Thatcher does. His Essential Services Act has been used to force back employees both in the private and public sectors. In no case has an "essential service" really been involved; the strikers have repeatedly offered to provide those services which are essential. Thatcher has repeatedly said no and sent everybody back to work. Now, according to Canadian Press interviews with Thatcher, the provincial government may ban strikes altogether. Such a move could help Thatcher in two ways: it might win him

rural support and serve as an additional carrot to American companies to exploit the province's resources.

The future under Thatcher will be bleak. Saskatchewan will continue to constitute a reserve pool of labor for the provinces to its east and west. Farmers' sons, unable to make a living on the farm, will be used as strike-breakers to enforce Thatcher's version of collective bargaining. The economy will remain extractive and in the hands of outside interests. Economic surplus will continue to leave the province. In short, the destiny of the people of Saskatchewan will be decided by and in the interests of monopolists rather than by and in the interests of the people themselves.

The solution to Saskatchewan's problems lies in regional development on the basis of social ownership. This could of course be achieved in the context of an independent socialist Canada. Clearly, however, the people of Saskatchewan cannot wait until Canadians as a whole can recognize the distortions caused by private and largely foreign ownership of the commanding heights of the economy. The farmers' union and the labor federation are led by men who recognize that only social ownership can reverse the economic fortunes of the province. It remains to be seen how militant these groups will be in pursuing policies that will challenge the economic forces that have decreed Saskatchewan's hinterland status. The reactionary nature of the Thatcher government makes its downfall a prerequisite to change. This raises two important questions. Can the NFU, the SFL and other such groups work together to convince the people of Saskatchewan that they face a common enemy whose chief tactic is to divide and conquer? Secondly, should they succeed in getting

the Liberals defeated, will they be willing to take steps necessary to force a chicken-hearted New Democratic Party government to challenge corporate power?

The answers to these questions are not important only to Saskatchewan. The dictates of corporate profits require increasing centralization of industries and population. The result is huge, unliveable cities characterized by unbreathable air, unsafe streets, huge pockets of poverty and a consumer ethic that requires more and more production leading to even less breathable air, larger pockets of pov-erty, more and more conformity, more and more alienation. John Robarts is planning to have 8,000,000 people in the Toronto area by the year 2000. Undoubtedly many of these people would come from the underdeveloped areas of the country to already over-developed Toronto. If Saskatchewan, with its socialist traditions, were to challenge the "right" of the corporations to decide its fate, perhaps a domino effect might occur in the other provinces. It may yet not be too late to save Canada from the fate that Robarts, Thatcher and the corporations seem to have planned for it.

WESTWARD HO FOR A NEW CAPITAL?

James Eayrs

James Eayrs is a professor at the University of Toronto. He has written extensively in the area of international relations.

Winnipeg should be the new capital for Canada's second century. Never mind about Ottawa, they've had the good life long enough.— W. A. C. Bennett, premier of British Columbia.

Premier Bennett's proposal, put forward last week in Manitoba at the meeting of provincial leaders there, has hardly stirred a cat, even among Winnipeggers. The response of Manitoba Premier Ed Schreyer — "Since he suggested Winnipeg, I found it hard to disagree with him" — seems more an attempt to humor a guest stricken by the heat than to offer a useful comment on a major constitutional innovation. All the same, the idea is not so wacky as it seemed. In a modified version, it merits consideration.

The premier is right for the wrong reason. It is not because of her prolonged enjoyment of the prerogatives of capital status that Ottawa should be stripped of some (not all) of her

Reproduced with permission from *Toronto Daily Star,* August 11, 1970.

official functions. A capital is not a popsicle (or joint) to be passed from mouth to mouth for the pleasure of the group. It is because of her poor performance. For more than a century she has had her chance to do for Canada what any capital ought to do for its country: become a place that looks good, like a showplace should; become a hospitable community for all who dwell or work or visit there. Ottawa has muffed her chance — on both these counts.

Natural setting

Despite a natural setting as glorious as any capital's, not much could be expected all at once of "a sub-Arctic lumbering town transformed by a stroke of Victoria's pen into a cockpit of malodorous politics" (an acerbic assessment of the 1880s). But after three-quarters of a century, surely something could be expected; and by the 1940s Ottawa had her admirers. "She is a small city," they would say (paraphrasing Daniel Webster on Dartmouth College), "but there are those who love her."

The loving ones were her privileged ones. Senior foreign diplomats, like Malcolm MacDonald, twittering of the birds of Brewery Creek. (That was before the planners plunked a six-lane bridge at the doorstep of his High Commission.) Senior civil servants, like Douglas LePan, "startled to hear a whitethroat singing from the maples near the statue of Sir Wilfrid Laurier while trying to stay awake through a long committee meeting in the Cabinet Room." Senior politicians, like Mackenzie King, whom the Country Club kept warm in winter: "We had cocktails in front of an open fire and then a round table dinner party. Light wines. Nice service. Stayed and had our coffee there."

Stench of sulphite

A seedier ambience prevails at lower depths, down in the bloated-underbelly of old Bytown, grubbier than Greber coud imagine, filled with file clerks and football fanatics. (A visitor told by a waiter to mark the celebrity behind him wheels round in anticipation of a minister of the Crown at least: it is Frank Clair, wolfing his egg-roll.) The birds of Clarence St., not Brewery Creek, utter their peculiar cry. The air reeks with the stench of sulphite. "A certain atmopshere flows about its walls," Archibald Lampman had reported from Ottawa in 1893, "borne upon the breath of the prevailing northwest wind, an intellectual elixir, an oxygenic essence. . . . " No wonder policy-makers in the days of Sir John Thompson rose with such alacrity to their duties; they could at least inhale without retching.

The federal government is partly at fault for Ottawa's inartistic quarters. By its authority exist those public buildings reared in "Sir Robert Borden Baroque" — the Royal Mint, the War Museum, the rest of the phony fortresses — and those still more characteristic structures built in "Canadian National Gothic." The federal government has also failed to use its bargaining power — deriving from a tax bill of $12 million a year — to induce municipal authorities to show a decent respect for the esthetics of their city.

But most blame attaches to those municipal authorities. The Whitton-Reid-Fogarty brand of local politics seems to have greenbacks, not greenbelts, as its obsession — one eye on the parish pothole, one eye on the parish porkbarrel, no eye on the master plan.

Graver by far than any physical blemishes are the scars of the spirit. "What is it about Ottawa," ask the authors of a recent study of *Bilingualism and Biculturalism in the Canadian House of Commons,* "that makes so many French-speaking MPs feel that French Canadians are not at home in the national capital?" Their reply, neither intuitive nor guesswork, being the tale told by their questionnaires, cites "the absence of bilingualism in the daily life of the city" as the fundamental factor, but cites as well "the coldness of the city, the lack of 'la gaieté,' good restaurants, and a cultural and artistic life." It's not just that French isn't spoken widely; hospitality isn't either.

Again, federal and local governments must share the blame for these Anglophonic attitudes. The federal authorities, reluctant to force change by pressure or by law, delinquent within their own jurisdiction (as when using non-French-speaking RCMP to patrol the capital's parkways), are at least trying to improve. That is more than can be said for the city of Ottawa. Its English-only street signs are symptomatic. So is its refusal to cooperate with the Royal Commission on Bilingualism and Biculturalism.

(The commission gets its own back by publishing the correspondence and comparing invidiously its obstructionist tone with the response of the mayor of Hull: "I hope that our humble contribution will be of use to you and congratulate you on the magnificent work.")

Co-capital would help

Dividing Ottawa's national duties and performing some of them elsewhere would create competition in biculturalism and the possibility of invidious comparisons of national capital performances. (Bennett's proposal to move the capital lock, stock and gargoyle would not.) Here is a solution which no royal commission study has felt able to consider. Out of the ensuing rivalry to fulfil their functions best, co-capitals could emerge of which all Canadians would feel proud and in which all would feel free.

For such a division of labor there is ample precedent — Amsterdam and The Hague, Cape Town and Pretoria, Rio and Brasilia, Islamabad and Dacca. Just what goes and just what stays is for negotiation. A sensible arrangement would keep Ottawa as the diplomatic capital, home to foreign embassies and those departments of the federal government whose business is mainly overseas; the less mobile national facilities (archives, library, museums) would also stay put. For Parliament and those departments whose business is mainly domestic, it would be westward ho.

Aim is empathy

To Winnipeg if necessary, but not necessarily to Winnipeg. That, too, is for negotiation. The new co-capital should be located in whatever community west of the Lakehead offers the best deal — not in land and buildings only, but in the red pavilion of the heart. The aim of the game is empathy. An irreversible commitment to the plea of the royal commission — "that the French and English languages have full equality of status, and that the full range of services and facilities provided to the public be available in both languages throughout the area" — should be the federal government's irreducible demand of any prospective western seat.

The Prime Minister ought to ponder a proposal that could make both western Canada and French Canada feel less alienated from Confederation. To help him ponder, in his office and at his ear is the namesake and maybe descendant of that statesman whose message to Queen Victoria settled her choice for the capital of British North America. Ivan Head comes from western Canada; a few strokes of his pen might transform yet another sub-Arctic town into a cockpit of even more malodorous politics than when occupied by Aberhard or Manning. He could negotiate on Sir Edmund Head's original dispatch, changing only a name or two: "It is most important therefore that western Canada should be made to feel its importance, and should connect its interests with the East. This object will be greatly promoted by the choice of . . . ." Would you believe Edmonton?

Part 3

Ontario is a state of mind, bounded on the east by a foreign language, on the north by wilderness, on the west by the hungry prairies, and on the south by another country.

Dorothy Duncan, Here's to Canada!, 1941.

WHAT IS A CANADIAN?

Eugene Cloutier

Eugene Cloutier is a French-Canadian writer.

What is a Canadian? Along the navigable waterway that links Lake Erie with Lake Huron, there is a tourist region to which Americans pour by way of Detroit and Windsor, one of the most important points of contact between Canada and the United States. It would be hard to say whether industry, agriculture or tourisms holds first position in the counties of Essex, Kent, and Lambton. If there is one province in Canada where all the resources of the economy blend into a harmonious whole it is Ontario. Seen from a certain angle, these elements influence one another and finally obey the same factors. And who can say at what moment agriculture or tourism break free of the old concepts to fall under the heading of industry? Industrial maturity perhaps comes on the day when you have industrialized everything. This is the impression I often had in Ontario.

Whether at the making of our Niagara wines, at the auctions of the tobacco producers at Tilsonburg or the automobile assembly-lines at Windsor, the rules of the game are the same. It is true that the presence of man can still preserve all its warmth as we saw at the Kitchener market. But on the whole I saw few essential differences between the industrial plants of Ontario and those of the large American states. This is the direction that all Quebec is taking at an accelerated rhythm, that Alberta has already taken, the direction the whole country will take in the long run. Our behaviour will be changed by it; it has already changed. I do not say whether this is for our good or our very great harm, I say only that we cannot escape it. Less than a century ago, the Windsor district was eighty per cent agricultural; today the metropolitan area includes two hundred thousand people and is eighty per cent industrial. The same seesaw is operating in all Canada. Ontario is far ahead of the rest of us. And this has resulted in a curious phenomenon.

In this province that I expected to find more English than Prince Edward Island or Newfoundland, at least in its traditions and its external aspects, I constantly met along my route a type that was not of England or of the United States and that might well be Canadian. But just as one is mistaken when one imagines the French of Quebec and the other provinces to be entirely bound up with France, I discovered here English and New Canadians who have developed for their province and their country an authentic sense of belonging, much as the French Canadians have come finally to feel American, and retain only sentimental and cultural bonds with their mother-country, and these so thin as to surprise you more than once.

A fact, a single little fact will suffice. At the time of the flag debate, everyone here believed that the abandonment of the Union Jack or the Red Ensign was a concession to Quebec. I was surprised to see our new flag floating everywhere in Ontario and it was rarely the subject of pleasantries or argument. New as it then was, it seemed to be already the object of a spontaneous cult. On my return to Montreal I saw it still floating timidly here and there, without attracting any attention other than jokes.

We are strange specimens of humanity and not always very easy to understand. But one certainty shines forth: we are no longer of France or of England or of Holland or of Hungary or of anywhere else. We are of a corner of North America, and in the two key provinces we are already of Canada, more often than not unknown to ourselves. And in the two key provinces, both on the English side and on the French side, we have fashioned ourselves a personality that does not resemble anything that is met with anywhere else, even in the United States.

ONTARIO

Claude Julien

Claude Julien is a French writer who has travelled extensively in Canada.

One-third of Canada's population lives between the Great Lakes and Hudson Bay and is responsible for half the industry of the country, 30 per cent of its mining, and 30 per cent of its agriculture. Ontario knows that it is the richest province and that without it the country's economy would founder. Annual *per capita* income is $2,011, compared with the national average of $1,734. Each year Ontario attracts over half (51 per cent) of the immigrants coming to Canada and 34 per cent of the capital investment. This assures it of a smoother and faster development, both of its population and of its economy, than any other province. Its mining production doubled from 1949 to 1963; its industrial production rose by 20 per cent between

Reprinted from *Canada: Europe's Last Chance*, by Claude Julien, by permission of The Macmillan Company of Canada Limited.

1956 and 1963. The unemployment rate is lower (3.8 per cent in 1963) than the national average (5.5 per cent) or the American average (5.7 per cent). Two-thirds of Canada's mechanical industry is in Ontario. The province is responsible for 90 per cent of Canada's production of electrical equipment.

Ontario's leaders, more than those of the other provinces, have a truly national outlook. Toronto knows that a good part of its industrial production is sold to the agricultural provinces and that their purchasing power depends on the harvest, on large wheat sales to the U.S.S.R. and to China, on federal protection to farmers, on credit regulations from Ottawa, *etc.* The provincialism of British Columbia or Saskatchewan is rarely found in Ontario, either among businessmen or among politicians. 'Our economic development depends not only on the federal government and Ontario, but on co-operation with the other provinces,' says Stanley Randall, Minister of Economics and Development. 'Some provinces have set up programs to encourage their own industrial development. These efforts could make a major contribution to the economic growth of Canada, as long as the advantages of specialization and of planning according to local resources are respected, and the waste of duplicated effort is avoided. If the development plans of the various provinces are mutually conflicting, we must work out a way of harmonizing them with an eye to the national interest.'[1]

The minister added: 'The economy of Ontario is more closely tied to the Canadian market than those of the other provinces, which means that it is in Ontario's vital interest to en-

courage the growth of the other parts of the country. For example, the Prairie farmer is a major factor in the increased demand this year for Ontario products, for the wheat sales to the communist countries have brought him extra revenue.'

None of this means that Ontario is not proud of its distinctive characteristics and does not sometimes yield to 'provincialism.' For example, part of Ontario's trade crusade has been to open bureaus in New York, Chicago, London, Dusseldorf, and Milan. Quebec, to mention only one other province, has 'delegations' in Paris, London, and New York. There is no theoretical reason why each of the ten provinces could not open offices in three or four foreign countries, in spite of the absurd waste of effort. In fact this process has already begun, and Ontario has pushed it the farthest, even though it has a strong voice in the federal government which has representatives in all of the countries that could possibly interest that province's economy.

But Ontario is less regional than the other provinces and has a greater sense of national reality and national interests. 'There are nine separatist provinces in this country, and one federalist, Ontario,' I was told by an English-speaking businessman from Manitoba. He was exaggerating slightly, for he was not taking into account New Brunswick, Nova Scotia, Prince Edward Island, and Newfoundland, the four poorest and least populated. They account for only 10 per cent of the nation's population, and their *per capita* income is much lower than the average. These four Cinderella provinces hold out their hands to Ottawa, and Ottawa plays with subsidies and sliding scales to keep them alive and in

[1]*Legislature of Ontario Debates*, April 23, 1964.

the federation. Separatism for them would be suicidal, and they intend to remain within Confederation. Yet, from the economic point of view these provinces are a liability and not an asset. Aware of their need to attract industry, they could well work for a better co-ordination of provincial efforts, but each puts out its own plans, on such a small scale that their viability is in question.

TORONTO

George Woodcock

George Woodcock has written many books in the fields of literature, politics, and travel. He lives in Vancouver.

Toronto is the epitome of the North American metropolis in its Canadian form. Montreal is bigger but also more cosmopolitan. In Toronto one encounters a peculiar combination of Scottish, English and American elements which affect not only the appearance of the town but also its life and its very atmosphere. Not many years ago Toronto was more British in sentiment even than Victoria, largely through the now diminished influence of the Orange Order and of White Anglo-Saxon Protestantism in general. That age has passed. The cultural links between Toronto and New York have strengthened, so that in many ways it is now the most 'American' of all Canadian cities. At the same time, post-World War II immigration has completely changed its view of Europe; an eighth of its people are now Italian by race.

Toronto is the most hated city in Canada. Its rivalry with Montreal is traditional, and Montrealers resent the fact that the balance of prosperity has shifted to the slightly smaller city; Bay Street, Toronto, is indisputably the financial capital of Canada. Business men in the Prairies, in Vancouver, in the Maritimes, bring the same accusations of attempted centralism against Toronto as are brought in by local politicians against Ottawa, and radicals see the city in the image which Stephen Leacock satirically presented when he portrayed the Torontonian élite in *Arcadian Adventures of the Idle Rich*, the other face of 'Toronto the Good'. The Augustan smugness of Toronto's academics arouses resentment in lesser Canadian universities, which often have better scholars, and the smart theatrical, artistic and literary journalists maintain an exasperating air of condescension toward other centres which are not lacking in genuine cultural life. The feeling between Vancouver and Toronto in this field is particularly sharp.

It is true that Toronto offers opportunities which attract many people of talent; it almost monopolizes the English-language publishing industry, and is the main centre of radio and television production. Much of its financial power comes from the fact that, apart from controlling through its Stock Exchange most of the mining investments in Canada's north, it lies in the heart of Canada's great industrial belt which runs along Lake Erie and Ontario and down the St. Lawrence as far as Quebec, and includes such important centres as the automobile town of Windsor and the great steel complex of Hamilton.

If Toronto were another Paris, or even another London, one might forgive its size and power. But it is, physically, an unattractive city; its centre was built fifty years ago in an unimaginative era of nonarchitecture, and has been little improved; its admirable lakefront has been wasted by bad planning; its sprawling suburbs lack the lush charm of Vancouver's, and, apart from a few Olympian districts of gardened mansions and some fashionable shopping streets where Victorian brick has been tastefully restored, there is little that attracts the eye, outside the Royal Ontario Museum, which houses one of the world's noblest collections of ancient Chinese artifacts. It is a city wholly dependent for its attraction on the life that its inhabitants inject into it, and here at least Toronto has become much more vivacious during the past decade, rather like one of those ugly girls who find themselves suddenly drifted off the shelf of neglect by the oddities of modern fashion.

LET'S TURN TORONTO AND MONTREAL INTO PROVINCES

Keith Davey

Keith Davey has played a prominent role in the Liberal party. He is now a senator and works in public relations.

Some 14 million Canadians have, for a variety of reasons, gravitated toward the cities. One in four of us lives either in Toronto or Montreal; more people live in each of these cities than live in the four Atlantic provinces put together. The 600,000 apartment-dwellers in the Toronto area almost equal the entire population of New Brunswick. One Toronto borough, North York, contains three times more people than live in all of Prince Edward Island. And Toronto's Italian and Polish communities together are approaching in numbers the entire population of Newfoundland.

The Fathers of Confederation, for all their admitted wisdom, could not possibly have foreseen Canada's dramatic population shift to the cities. How could they have been expected to understand some of the enormous problems that now confront urban Canada? Some of these problems — most notably the staggering tax burden — the great cities have in common with Canadians everywhere. Urban poverty is, perhaps, more soul-destroying, more miserable than rural. The housing crisis, as distinct from

the housing shortage, is an urban phenomenon, as are clogged and inadequate expressway. Air pollution is a national problem, but only in Toronto and Montreal has it reached outrageous proportions.

These uniquely urban problems are compounded by political and economic superstructures that are often, at worst, obsolete and, at best, detrimental to the interests of the city dweller. As creatures of their respective provinces, Toronto and Montreal must work within the framework of provincial legislatures structured in favor of rural interests over urban. The Ontario Municipal Board, for example, which was created more than 60 years ago, continues to confirm the jurisdiction of provincially appointed bureaucrats over Toronto's popularly elected municipal representatives. It has become in many ways an intolerable situation.

Perhaps a short-term solution is in the advent of the party system at the municipal level. In Toronto this will result this December in more and better candidates, far greater voter involvement and a choice between programs rather than personalities as in the past. It is interesting, incidentally, that opposition to the proposal

Reprinted with permission of Senator Keith Davey from *Maclean's*, August 1969.

that the Liberal Party enter municipal politics came substantially from rural Ontario. It may be that the rest of Ontario isn't ready for such change, but Metropolitan Toronto desperately needs this kind of reform.

However, this is at best a stopgap solution, because, as things are, no mayor of Toronto or chairman of Metropolitan Toronto can effectively solve Toronto's financial crisis, strangled as it is in provincial red tape.

I am indebted to Both Prime Minister Trudeau and, more indirectly, Norman Mailer for an idea that has much merit: that urban areas in Canada become separate provinces when their populations exceed two million. Mr. Trudeau referred to the city state in his remarks at the campaign love-in last June in Toronto's Nathan Phillips Square. Mailer, along with his sidekick Jimmy Breslin, advocated separate statehood for New York City in his recent quest for the Democratic Party mayoralty nomination.

I think Canadians should carefully examine the possibility of making Toronto and Montreal "City Provinces" — but provinces with all the power of, say, Prince Edward Island or, for that matter, of Quebec and Ontario.

This proposed expression of creative federalism should not be confused with either isolationism or separatism; neither Toronto or Montreal could survive as separate entities. The prosperity of each is inextricably linked with the prosperity of the rest of the country. As "have" provinces, each would, of course, contribute to the "have-not" sections of Canada. Indeed, there would be great additional benefits for the rest of Ontario and Quebec, which could then give attention more directly to such dramatic concerns as northern development and rural poverty.

For the City Provinces there would be at least three enormous advantages, each of which would facilitate an attack on major areas of urban concern.

First, the City Provinces would raise their own money by levying their own taxes and by making their own financial arrangements with Ottawa. Because they had raised their own revenues. City Provinces would be able to spend the money to achieve a degree of "home rule" and could break out of the triple-tiered tax jungle.

Second, an entire layer of government would be peeled off. Existing essential services would be maintained but blended into an overall urban pattern. Obviously, such City Provinces would have to develop an effective working relationship with the provinces out of which they were carved, but their most direct relationship would be with the federal government. (Perhaps the existence of such City Provinces might have solved the dilemma Paul Hellyer found himself in when his zest for action became entangled with constitutional reality.)

Third, the creation of such City Provinces would solve the amalgamation dilemma by setting the stage for neighborhood councils that would provide far more meaningful local representation than is possible in the existing borough structure. Moreover, they would facilitate participatory democracy.

I raise the idea here as one worth examining. In my view, the converting of Toronto and Montreal into City Provinces would improve the quality of life for more than one-quarter of all Canadians and indirectly benefit all the rest.

FACTS BEHIND THE TERROR

Dian Cohen

Dian Cohen lives in Montreal and writes on economic affairs for the Toronto Daily Star *on a regular basis.*

Pierre Laporte, minister of labor in the Quebec government, is minister of unemployment to the men who kidnapped him.

It is disturbing that the English media, not only in English Canada but in Quebec as well, have chosen to ignore the fact that behind FLQ actions lie some very real grievances.

It is perhaps easier to believe that the FLQ is a small group of criminal madmen than to accept the possibility that the anger and frustration which gives rise to such violent actions may fairly accurately reflect the feelings of a much larger group of French Canadians.

It is more convenient to slough off separatists, as Prime Minister Pierre Trudeau did after the Quebec election last spring, as just a "bunch of discontented Quebeckers," or to discount political terrorists as "bandits and outlaws," than to explain in meaningful terms to the one in 11 Quebeckers presently out of work why he is likely to remain so.

Here are some facts:

— In the past 15 years, Quebec has never come anywhere close to full employment; unemployment has never been lower than 4 per cent, even in summer, and has frequently been as high as 15 per cent.

— While Quebeckers comprise a little over one quarter of Canada's labor force, fully 41 per cent of Canadians out of work last year lived in Quebec.

— Historically, unemployment in Quebec has been 20 to 40 per cent higher than average unemployment in Canada, and 50 to 100 per cent higher than average unemployment in Ontario.

— Seasonally adjusted unemployment in Canada last year was 4.7 per cent. It was 6.9 per cent in Quebec.

— Nearly all people without work in Quebec are French Canadian.

— The average number of unemployed people in Quebec last year was 158,000. Of these, 65,000, or 42 per cent, were under 25.

— The average income of English-speaking workers in Quebec is 40 per cent higher than that of French-speaking workers.

— The Bilingual and Bicultural Commission concluded in 1964 that French-speaking employees, who represent 70 per cent of Quebec's labor force, hold 82 per cent of jobs in the $5,000-$6,000 bracket. English-speaking employees who are 30 per cent

Reprinted with permission, *Toronto Daily Star,* October 16, 1970.

of the labor force, hold 77 per cent of the jobs in the $15,000 bracket.

It is clear that a young French Canadian has an excellent chance of being unemployed — greater, certainly, than a young English Canadian.

One can with some confidence say that revolutionaries are not overly-concerned with the "whys" of Quebec's economic disadvantages. They undoubtedly do not want to hear about the lower educational levels, the lower levels of capital investment, the high concentration of low-growth industries in Quebec. It is not all Ottawa's fault. But a good part of it is.

When Robert Bourassa was elected premier last April, a great many English Canadians heaved a sigh of relief and comforted themselves that separatism was dead.

But as one French Canadian journalist wrote shortly after the election: "It would be a grave mistake to think that Rene Levesque's defeat will stop (independentists) from promoting the idea of independence. Quebec has not suddenly become a paradise of fraternity, an island of peace. The ferment of revolution, of chaos, is as alive in our collectivity as it is in many places in the world.

"If Bourassa does not find jobs — he promised 100,000 — for young Quebeckers, troubles and violence will start all over again. If his economic theory does not reap new investments and stabilize our financial situation, those who trusted his flair for finance will turn against him."

The FLQ, and other separatists who do not condone terrorist methods, were never for Bourassa. And current statistics, which reveal that unemployment is near record proportions in Quebec, clearly spell trouble for the Bourassa government.

The economic forces at the root of slow employment growth are being generated by Ottawa. Not even the most enterprising provincial government could make headway in the face of federal monetary and fiscal policies still more concerned with inflation than with unemployment.

Employment in Quebec increased by 85,000 in 1965, and by 104,000 in 1966, the year Canada was preparing for its centennial birthday and Quebec was building Expo '67.

In the following three years, 1967, '68 and '69, only 116,000 new jobs were created. In 1968, a low was hit when only 2,000 new jobs came into existence. At the same time, unemployment in Quebec has risen from 109,000 in 1967 to 145,000 in 1968 to 158,000 in 1969 to well over 200,000 so far in 1970.

Finance Minister Benson said earlier this week that unemployment will fall during 1971.

Will the young French Canadian believe him? And even if he should do so, will it change his own individual plight? Probably not.

EDITOR'S NOTE:

A more comprehensive understanding of the situation in Quebec is provided by *Canadian/ Canadien*, another book in the Issues for the Seventies series.

Part 4

We are few in numbers; our country is but a narrow tract, surrounded by populous States; and we have no prospect of distinction — I had almost said of future safety — but from high mental and moral cultivation, infusing into every branch of industry such a degree of intellectual vigour as shall insure success, multiply population, and endow them with productive power.

Joseph Howe, 1843.

CAN UNION SAVE
THE MARITIMES?

Walter Stewart

Walter Stewart is an Associate Editor of
Maclean's *magazine.*

Murray Hubbard is 58, a slender, grey whippet of a man with the large, gnarled hands and the season-seamed face of someone who has been farming hard all his life. He lives with his wife Gwendolen in a battered old farmhouse on the tree-shrouded hills above Debec, in western New Brunswick, not far from the St. John River valley. He raises sheep and Christmas trees, loves flowers — he used to raise them, too, but the sheep kept eating them—and spends whatever time he can spare, reading. He is a thoughtful man, clever and hardworking. He has been clever and hard-working all his life, but it hasn't done much good. Last year, the income from his 350-acre farm came to $6,359; it cost $6,100, of which $1,000 was depreciation on equipment, to run the place. Murray Hubbard is trapped in the Maritimes economy.

Amedee Gallant is 54 but, with his straight black hair and sturdy, suntanned features, looks younger. He is an inshore fisherman at Cape Egmont, along the low and windswept shore of Prince Edward Island, not far from Summerside. He learned the trade from his father; he is good at it, and enjoys it, enjoys the quiet morning when he turns his 40-foot lobster boat out to meet the dawn breaking over Northumberland Strait, enjoys the evening run back, after a hard day of hauling on the rocking sea, with a catch gleaming wetly from the bottom of his boat. Gallant lives with his wife and three of his nine children — the others have grown up and left home — in a small, spotless house just inland. They get along, but the going gets rougher every year. Last year, Gallant earned $4,600, paid $1,200 for a helper, and was left with $3,400 to run his boat and house and take care of his family. Looking ahead, he can see only worse times coming, for the lobster catch grows leaner with each passing season. Like Hubbard, Gallant is caught in an economy that doesn't seem to work.

George Butts is 47 and, like Gallant, looks younger than his years. His hair is a light brown, his eyes a clear blue, and he moves with the vigor of a man who has worked with his hands and back and legs all his life. Butts is a coal miner, as was his father before him. For 28 years, he worked in the same black pit, No. 20 Colliery at Glace Bay, Nova Scotia. He began as a driver on a horse-drawn pit wagon, worked up to be the operator of a Joy Miner, a huge machine that claws coal from the mine wall and loads it on to railway cars in a single operation. Butts was among the elite in No. 20, for only two men on each shift could operate a Joy Miner, and he was paid top wages — $24.86 a shift — enough to support himself, his wife and the four of his nine children still at home in the small duplex at Birch Grove, just outside Glace Bay. Then, quite recently, No. 20 Colliery closed down, in the retrenchment that has become necessary for the survival of the Cape Breton coal industry. Butts was moved to another pit, where the pay begins at $18 a shift. There are no Joy Miners in No. 26 Colliery, so he will have to learn a new job. He doesn't know how long this pit will last, but guesses maybe five years at the most. Then he will have to find something else to do — although there is nothing else he is trained to do — or take early retirement, live on a pinched pension and sit around, like so many Cape Breton miners, waiting for something better to happen.

Murray Hubbard, Amedee Gallant and George Butts are the three strongest arguments I know for the political union of the Maritime provinces. All are men of energy, intelligence and skill, and all are finding that energy, intelligence and skill are not tools enough to wring prosperity from the land where they live. None of them earns what a Montreal plumber or a Hamilton steelworker would call a decent living, yet they work in three of the basic industries of their region. I have picked them, not because they are typical, but be-cause they are better-than-typical in their skills. Hubbard is a knowledgeable farmer, and president of the New Brunswick Sheep-Breeders' Association; Gallant took the highest lobster catch in the co-op he belongs to in 1967, and the second-highest last year; Butts was among the handful of specialists in No. 20 Colliery.

These men face the problems faced by their fathers and grandfathers and, without some basic restructuring of the area, the same or worse problems will face their children and grandchildren (unless, like so many of the best in the Maritimes, those children and grandchildren simply say to hell with it, and move out). Hence the plea for union now.

Maritime Union is a proposal that Nova Scotia, New Brunswick and Prince Edward Island come together as a single province, with one capital, one legislature, one civil service and one set of laws. Today the Atlantic provinces appear to Ottawa as three little groups of lawmakers who cannot agree on what they want; they speak with a scattering of shrill voices to a federal government already assailed by other and more powerful calls. Until the region speaks with a single voice, it will have trouble getting its requests heard. The three provinces tentatively recognized the point in March 1968, when they commissioned a Maritime Union study to look into the pros and cons of merger. That study will report next spring. It will set forth, in heavily charted detail, what union might mean in every field from education to truck licensing.

Part of the case for union is his-toric — when John A. Macdonald and seven colleagues from the Province of Canada arrived in Charlottetown on September 1, 1864, and set in train the talks that led to Confederation, they came as gate-crashers to a conference that had been called to discuss Maritime Union. The tariff barriers Canada threw up after Confederation cut off the Maritimes from their natural markets in the United States — and a century of widening disparity with the rest of Canada began. For 42 years per capita incomes in the region have been the nation's lowest and though politicians have complained, they have done it with little hope of change. Much of the area has come to believe that it's always been poor and always will be and that's the end of it. The first and most important effect of a merger now would be to throw off this ancient stink of defeat and begin again.

There is a more contemporary spur to union. The region desperately needs modern business practice. At present, for example, a New Brunswick trucking company must pay double taxation if it can't prove that its drivers bought enough gas in Nova Scotia to cover their travels in that province. Union would do away with such ludicrous imposts.

It would not, by itself, solve the problems of Hubbard, Gallant and Butts. But it would affect them. By welding three scattered economies together, it would provide better markets and a magnet for industry — more jobs for those whom farming and fishing can no longer sustain. The political muscle that could be exerted on behalf of the nearly 1.5 million people of a united Maritimes — it would be Canada's fifth-largest province — would be far greater than the combined muscle of today's Nova Scotia (762,000 people), New Brunswick (626,000) and PEI (110,000). It would mean better public service for Hubbard, Gallant and Butts — paid for from savings made possible by ending the pointless duplication of provincial governments. The Maritimes today groans under the weight of more officialdom than any area in Canada — 136 provincial legislators, 38 cabinet ministers, three lieutenants-governor and 24,106 provincial civil servants look to the needs of a population two thirds the size of Metropolitan Toronto. The Atlantic Provinces' Economic Council has calculated that if the Maritimes ratio of civil servants (one for every 61.6 citizens) could be brought down to the ratio for the rest of Canada (one for 106.1) the annual saving in salaries would be $38 million. That money could help find better markets for Murray Hubbard or a better job for his son.

Murray Hubbard's father, an Englishman, moved to Debec from Philadelphia when Hubbard was two, because the American firm he worked for wanted him to take out U.S. citizenship. He became a farmer, and his only child followed him on to the land after progressing as far as one month into grade seven at the Speerville School, just down the road.

Despite the lack of formal learning, Hubbard has given himself a first-rate education, and likes to lard his conversation with historical references and pertinent quotations. My favorite of his quotations is not, admittedly, high toned; it came from a discussion of prohibition in the U.S., and went like this:

Four-and-twenty Yankees,
All very dry,
Crossed the Yankee border
To get Canadian rye.
When the rye was open,
They began to sing,
"To hell with Calvin Coolidge,
God Save The King."

At first, life was prosperous enough, and Hubbard can remember when 17 families, most of them large ones, lived along the Speerville road. "Now there's only one family that can get by without outside help, and that's us." On top of the problem common to all Canadian farmers — the fact that costs of production go up faster than the price of farm products — Maritimers face the special difficulties of high transportation charges and vigorous competition in the central Canadian market, while the route to their natural market, in the U.S., is beset by tariff barriers. Hubbard's life has been spent, as much of his father's life was spent, running hard to stand still.

When he married, his wife brought a dowry of two purebred Oxford ewes, and Hubbard went into the sheep business. Now he has a flock of 250 adults and 200 lambs, whose wool and meat provide his main income. It's not enough, although both he and his wife work long hours. "We're up against something we can't lick . . . Canadian Pacific can off-load New Zealand lamb in Toronto cheaper than I can put it there, no matter how hard I work, or how cheaply I live."

Hubbard's son, John, 23, wants no part of this unequal struggle. With his wife and daughter, he lives at Meductic, 10 miles away, and drives a truck for a living. "If sheep ran on gas, he'd be a humdinger," says Hubbard, "but he's just not interested in this farm, and I can't blame him." Truck-driving doesn't hold much future either, but there is nothing else.

Amedee Gallant is an Acadian, whose French-speaking people have lived along PEI's west shore for generations. His grandfather ran the farm just across the road, but his father took to the sea and Gallant followed him when he was 16 and through grade eight.

He is a slow-speaking man, careful, neat and patient. He catches lobster in the summer, herring in the spring and fall (it was selling for six dollars for a 200-pound barrel when I was at Cape Egmont) and, whenever he can, he rakes Irish moss from the seabed. This is a kind of seaweed used in medicines and in the making of ice cream; it brings three cents a pound. In the winter, when there is no fishing, he works on his traps, takes on odd jobs as a carpenter, or lives on unemployment insurance. Last winter, he went back to school. "They started this retraining business, where the government pays you to study, so I did that. I'd rather go to school and get $64 a week than stay home and get $36 on the unemployment."

Gallant upgraded his education from grade eight to grade 10, catching up with his daughter Jenny, 16, two years behind Florence, 17. He doesn't know what he'll do with his new knowledge; he could go to Charlottetown and take a welding course, but there are no welding jobs in the area, and besides, "We're fishermen here and we like fishing and we're going to have to starve before we quit."

Florence knows what to do with her diploma, however; she's getting out, to Toronto, where two brothers and two sisters have already fled. "I don't blame them," says Gallant, "there is nothing for them here."

Those last six words could make a Maritimes hymn. The best and brightest of the young people grow up, look around, and pull out, and the trend is getting worse. Between 1951 and 1956, an average of 7,400 people fled the Atlantic provinces every year; between 1956 and '61, the figure reached 11,800, and in the next five years, it nearly doubled, to 20,800. The exiles were those the area could least afford to lose: 81 percent of those who left in the 1961-66 period were under 29; in those five years the Atlantic provinces lost 64,000 young people between the ages of 15 and 29.

To Gallant, these remorseless figures are not numbers on a page, they are members of his family scattering across the land. His one remaining son, Louis, 13, will probably go to university; probably, if he does, he will leave, too, for in the Maritimes higher learning is often merely a form of preflight training. The circle is a vicious one — because the economy is sluggish, the young people move out; because they move out, the economy continues to be sluggish. Maritime Union would break this circle if it means, as the Atlantic Provinces Economic Council claims it would mean, greater efficiency, greater incentive and greater opportunities at home. "Nobody who lives here wants to go," Gallant told me, "but they have to have some reason for staying."

When George Butts was a youngster, his father told him, "Whatever you do, don't be like me; stay out of the mine." The easy way to follow that advice was to leave the area, and seven of Butts' brothers and sisters did so. He stayed, because he likes the rugged country of his birth, likes hunting and fishing and the quiet pace. After school — he got as far as grade eight — he tried farming, but that didn't work, tried a job with the Department of Transport, but that wasn't steady and so, at 19, he went into the mine, driving a horse for $3.64 a day. Mine work is hard, dirty, sometimes brutal; Butts has broken two bones in his hand and two in his feet in accidents (he enjoyed the convalescences, away from the grimy pit) and once, two years ago, a man was killed within a few feet of him by a run-away ore cart.

"It's a no-good life," Butts says. "Nobody would go into it if there was anything else."

For many Cape Bretoners, there isn't even mining, and any visitor to Glace Bay or Sydney can see the men who used to work in closed-down pits sitting in the beer halls, some talking, some reading newspapers, some simply staring at the wall and wondering what went wrong. Despite everything, Butts' son Terry, who is 25, has gone into the pit. What else is there to do?

John Stuart Mill once wrote, "When the object is to raise the permanent condition of the people, small means do not merely produce small effects, they produce no effect at all." The heart of the dilemma facing George Butts' family is that none but small means have ever been applied to the area where they live. What is needed is new industry to replace the mines, but industry is not drawn to the marginal economy of the Maritimes, and that economy can only be strengthened if it is efficiently run, tightly integrated and regionally planned. Provincial boundaries stand in the way of all these aims. Although no fewer than 150 agencies have been established to promote cooperation in the Atlantic region, the system breaks down when it comes to such vital matters as placing industry where it will most benefit the entire area, and helping it to operate efficiently wherever it is located. "If all our vaunted cooperation worked," asks Arthur C. Parks, chief econo-

mist for the Atlantic Provinces Economic Council, "would we be in the pickle we're in today?"

Firms coming into the Maritimes are located by the tug of local politics and the size of the bribes each province can offer in tax concessions, land grants and low-interest loans. The results are often unhappy for both the industy and the province. When Bathurst Marine Ltd. couldn't get the favors it wanted from New Brunswick, it decamped to PEI, where it obtained generous concessions, then failed, leaving the province heavily in debt. When Clairtone Sound Corporation decided to set up on the east coast, company officers ran simultaneous bargaining sessions with New Brunswick and Nova Scotia, until New Brunswick Premier Louis Robichaud found out what was going on and broke off negotiations. Clairtone set up in Nova Scotia with massive government support, but little success. Eventually, the province took over administration of the firm, which last year lost nine million dollars. The point is not that either of these companies should have gone to Glace Bay to give Terry Butts a job, but that industry must be located according to the laws of economic sense not provincial rivalry, or there will be few jobs for anyone.

However they arrive, firms trying to do business in the Maritimes must follow a bewildering array of rules to reach each of three small markets. There are different sales taxes, health regulations and trucking laws in each province. Maritime Co-operative Services Ltd., a large wholesaling firm, was forced to put sliding axles on two semitrailers, so their length could be adjusted to meet differing weight rules in each province. MCS must also maintain three separate inventories of such commonplace items as margarine and pesticides because of varying standards. Three sets of labor laws, incorporation procedures and tax-collection methods also add to the headache. MCS is not about to pull out — its roots are here — but how many potential industries, in the light of such expensive harassments, look over the Maritimes and pass on by?

APEC economist Arthur Parks argues that parochialism is a brake on the Maritime economy, and that only political union will give the area a chance to live up to its potential. "Union won't solve all our problems," he says, "but at least it's a start."

Will that start ever be made? I believe it will, though not easily and not soon. Five years ago, when I first looked at Maritime Union, I found that, in general, New Brunswick was for it, Nova Scotia was against it (as the most prosperous province, Nova Scotia fears it might be pulled down by the others) and PEI viewed the project with massive indifference. Since then, the increasing difficulties of the area and the continuing migrations of its people have made union more palatable, if only as a last resort. There is a gradually growing feeling that union can't do much harm, and might do some good.

At the moment, the business community is marginally in favor and the political community marginally opposed. The businessmen are concerned with efficiency. Harrison McCain, joint general manager of McCain Foods Ltd., at Florenceville, NB, told me, "It makes economic sense, and that's good enough for me." The politicians are concerned about their jobs. A united legislature will mean fewer seats and more competition for them, and, although they don't like to say so out loud, few of them are willing to try their luck in a bigger pond. (Two notable exceptions are New Brunswick Premier Louis Robichaud and Opposition Leader Richard Hatfield, both supporters of union.)

All that is needed to upset this tug of war between business and politics is one new factor, and there are two of them. The first is the impact of a new generation of voters, impatient with old ways and more than willing to try the experiment of union. The second is the Maritime Union Study itself. Most Maritimers are conservative by nature; they want to be shown. Through the publicity it is generating by its work,

the study is showing them. If, when it reports next spring, the study favors union — and my guess is that it will, either directly or by inference — that endorsement should be enough to tip the scales.

There will still be many problems to face, from the choice of a capital (one wag has suggested that it be placed on a barge and towed from province to province) to a name for the new province (suggested so far: Maritopia, Atlantica, Atlanta, Acadia and Nova Brunsland), but within five years, I believe, the Maritimes will be on the way to finishing the conference John A. Macdonald interrupted in 1864.

PERIL AND GLORY

Joseph Smallwood

Joseph Smallwood is the Premier of Newfoundland.

I have strong feelings on the development of federal-provincial relations. My favorite allusion is to Procrustes who welcomed travellers to his castle and offered them a bed for the night.

They had to fit the bed. If they were too short, he stretched them. If they were too long, he lopped off their feet. But they had to fit his bed.

To far too great an extent, the government of Canada follows the same policy, Procrustes' bed policy. They make all 10 provinces fit that bed and all provinces cannot fit the bed.

They don't follow that policy as much as they did. Not because of Newfoundland but contemporaneously with our membership in the Canadian family, there has been a growing tendency in Ottawa to admit frankly and to get the more favored

Reproduced with permission of The Hon. J. R. Smallwood, Premier of Newfoundland and Labrador.

parts of Canada to admit frankly, that the Procrustes' bed policy is wrong. There has been a growing tendency to admit that you must abandon the old sterile idea that we cannot do this for any province unless we do it for all provinces. We cannot do this for this province or that province because it would be unfair to do it for one or two and not do it for all. We cannot do anything unless we're prepared to do it equally for all.

That idea is slightly abandoned now compared with 15 or 18 years ago and certainly compared with 25 or 30 years ago. There are a good many examples of legislation in recent years quite openly and unashamedly slanted in favor of this or that province, particularly the four Atlantic provinces. These provinces have been on the right end of actions taken by the government of Canada.

There are half a dozen examples of it. These are to the good. These are excellent. These are absolutely the right thing for the government of Canada to do.

It seems to me there's got to be a lot more of this. There's got to be much more frank and unashamed abandonment of the theory that all provinces have to be treated equally and alike.

Anatole France said the law in its majesty equality treats the millionaire and pauper alike; it forbids them both to sleep under the public bridge. The law is impartial and the two are treated impartially.

Whenever the government of Canada said to the 10 provinces, "We will pay half the cost of doing this or doing that or doing the other in your provinces if you will pay half the cost." Ontario said, "Fine, we'll take you up on that." Prince Edward Island and Newfoundland said with less alacrity, "Yes, all right, we'll try."

But where does Newfoundland and where does P.E.I. get the money to match Ottawa's money? This apparent fairness, this apparent even handed justice is cruelly unjust. It's the Procrustes' bed policy.

Again, natural resources are provincial in jurisdiction and title and right. But provinces are unequal, very unequal, in their ability to search for natural resources, to discover them, to blueprint them, to develop them. They are all very unequal in their ability to do these things and therefore very unequal in the amount of natural resource development they've got. This in turn deepens and widens the gulf between the provinces.

Yet Ottawa has always, and still to this day in that particular matter, followed the Procrustes policy of even handed, majestic impartiality between the provinces. It does so by carrying on federal works of an investigative character, surveys, mineral surveys, geological, geodetic surveys, marine, forest surveys, and what have you.

They seem to think it would be very wrong for them just to stop all further surveys, not spend another federal dollar in Ontario or Quebec or British Columbia or Alberta — but rather to concentrate all of their expenditures, every last dollar, for the next 10 or 20 years in those provinces which have been least able to find their own money to do that work, and least able to entice outside capital in, outside companies in, to spend money on these purposes.

I haven't had many but I've had a few disappointments in our act of Confederation, and one of the main ones I have felt is precisely that. It has always seemed to me that it would be sound statesmanship, sound federal, sound Canadian, overall to Canada, statesmanship, for the federal government to have spent two to three hundreds of millions of dollars in these last 18 years in the four Atlantic provinces.

Again, just as they would recognize the need of the four Atlantic provinces being paramount in this field and outweighing all the rest of Canada put together, so within this limited part of Canada, these four provinces, they would recognize Newfoundland's need. They would follow the same principle through. They wouldn't try to treat the four Atlantic provinces with majestic equality, that having started, having conceded in the first place that these four provinces are in much greater need of federal activity in that matter than the rest of Canada, so within the four they would recognize that Newfoundland's need was greater than that of the other three.

It seems to me they have been dogged by the feeling that they mustn't do anything for one that they don't do equally for all others. As I say, they are getting away gradually, here and there, in a few fields, from it. Still, the policy of majestic impartiality is carried out to a disappointing extent.

It seems to me, therefore, that the policy of the government of Canada should be most assuredly, most definitely, the Robin Hood policy of taking from the rich and giving to the poor, using the revenue collected from the main sources of revenue in Canada to speed up development in the other parts of Canada. This should be a quite deliberate policy. They should never cease to look for ways of doing it. It wouldn't take too

many years before all of the underdeveloped provinces were as developed as they could be, relatively speaking, as developed as highly and intensely, as they were capable of being.

At that point, you would have those provinces cease to be "have not" provinces and become "have" provinces. Surely from a Canadian standpoint, the standpoint of Canada as a nation, it would be better if they were all "have" provinces. Surely it would be better if all provinces contributed more to Ottawa than they drew from Ottawa, not as now where some contribute more to Ottawa than they get back and others contribute far less than they get back and the surplus of one be used to help the other. That's the case now.

This could go on forever at the present pace without providing the remedy. If they step it up considerably, they might in 10 or 20 or 30 years raise the standards in the "have not" provinces to the point where they wouldn't need to be doing that or wouldn't need nearly so much to be doing it. It seems to me that that ought to be the attitude, the whole approach of the Parliament and government of Canada to the matter of the provinces.

How can we all, all 10 provinces and all of our people, get along better with each other?

We debate. We argue. We declaim. We show off. We get angry.

One can hope that out of it all will come more understanding.

I'm not so sure that the great vast public of Canada is gravely or deeply or frequently concerned with all this. I think most people are just going about their business, their own pleasures, their own enjoyments, their families, loafing and having leisure, and relaxing and working and travelling.

I don't think the average Canadian is going around even as much as giving this a thought. I think it's a very limited number of people who are worried about it.

TRUDEAU PLAN POURS MILLIONS INTO MARITIMES

Anthony Westell

Anthony Westell is the Ottawa editor of the Toronto Daily Star.

OTTAWA — Standing on a windswept shopping plaza in suburban St. John's, Nfld., on a cold spring afternoon two years ago, Pierre Elliott Trudeau proclaimed a new economic aid plan to bring a fair share of Canadian prosperity to the hardpressed people of the eastern provinces.

As the election crowd pressed hopefully around him, the new Prime Minister explained how he would organize a massive transfer of resources from the rich provinces to the poor, much as the United States poured its Marshall aid dollars into postwar Europe to bring about the miracle of economic recovery and development.

Building spirit of nationhood

Trudeau declared this to be one of his top priorities in strengthening national unity, ranking with constitutional reform to reconcile French and English, and it became a major election promise — part of his just society.

Today, millions of dollars in federal funds are flowing into eastern Quebec and the Atlantic provinces in a rising river of aid which is one of the most far-reaching national development efforts since Confederation.

The objective is not merely to raise living standards in the east, to provide jobs and opportunity in place of welfare and limited horizons.

It is, also, to spread economic development across Canada in a way which will build the spirit of nationhood and reduce the disruptive pressures of population and industrialization on Toronto, Montreal and the other exploding urban centres.

Cities undergo modernization

From Three Rivers, Que., to the outports of Newfoundland, federal funds are:

— Building municipal roads, schools, sewer systems and even recreational facilities to modernize the cities and make them more attractive to industry.

— Providing millions in risk capital to businesses ranging from multinational giants such as International Business Machines to Chinese food freezers, to create new jobs and payrolls.

— Moving the rural poor from isolated communities to new centres where they can enjoy better homes, schools and social services, and experimenting with job training techniques to give them a chance in the new industrial state.

— Constructing attractions including historic villages and championship golf courses to lure tourist dollars into the regional economy.

The whole development program is not yet a guaranteed success. There have been many previous attempts to stimulate economic growth and rural reform, launched with high hopes but enjoying only marginal and temporary success.

The ARDA (Agricultural Rehabilitation and Development Act of 1961) became a more broadly based rural aid scheme in 1966, followed by FRED (Fund for Rural Economic Development) the same year.

The Atlantic Development Board was set up in 1962 to foster growth in the region, and there have been a series of plans offering tax concessions and outright grants to industries establishing in slow-growth regions.

But the Trudeau government's campaign is certainly the most vigorous, comprehensive and best financed so far.

Social reform

For the first time there is a Department of Regional Economic Ex-

pansion, bringing all federal efforts under one command.

The importance of the department is emphasized by the fact that the minister in charge is Trudeau's friend and close political associate, Jean Marchand, a former union leader with a deep personal commitment to social justice. His deputy is Tom Kent who became one of the influential civil service mandarins after serving for years as brains-truster and principal aide to prime minister Lester Pearson.

With a headquarters staff of close to 400 — one of the smaller, more select Ottawa bureaucracies — in the top nine floors of a modern office tower, these two men direct the campaign to modernize a major sector of the Canadian economy. But they see it not so much as an exercise in economics as a matter of Canadian nationalism and social reform.

Economic inequality strains national unity when Maritimers complain bitterly that they have not had a fair deal out of Confederation because they make only $7 of income for every $10 enjoyed by the average Canadian.

This sort of comparative poverty, with unemployment up to twice the national average, encourages embittered Quebeckers to support separatism as a protest movement.

Marchand and Kent have the job of proving to Eastern Canadians, English and French, that Confederation works for them too.

Trudeau has given them growing funds and a new strategy of development. At a time when budgets of most federal departments are frozen, or under severe restraint, spending on regional economic expansion is rising from $233.6 million last year to $353.6 million this year, and is forecast to continue growing rapidly for several years ahead.

The new strategy provides that instead of concentrating the development campaign on backward rural areas, as in the past, the campaign should now centre on selected cities — the growth centres which, hopefully, will spread their own prosperity into surrounding districts and upgrade the whole regional economy..

The Star spent three weeks examining Trudeau's Marshall plan, at Ottawa headquarters and in the Maritimes, to describe the quiet revolution in the East.

U. S. investment

The study has produced impressive evidence that at last a determined effort is being made to raise the slow-growth regions closer to the prosperity enjoyed in the rich provinces. But it has also uncovered policy puzzlers.

While there is steadily climbing concern about the existing extent of foreign ownership in Canada, and uneasiness about the role of powerful multi-national corporations, the Department of Regional Economic Expansion is actively seeking and subsidizing more U.S. investment.

Some of the biggest grants have gone to the wealthiest corporations to persuade them to locate in less developed areas of Canada: $6,000,000 to IBM; $4,100,000 to Control Data Ltd.; more than $1,000,000 to Boeing Aircraft, to name a few.

The department does not now ask the nationality of a company which qualified for a grant. Nor is there any reason why it should under existing federal policy.

Over-industrialized

But if the cabinet ever decides to take a stand against foreign capital, the present regional development program would be badly damaged and might collapse.

A second doubt concerns the whole objective of maximizing industrial development. There is a growing school of thought that North America may already be over-industrialized, producing all the problems of pollution, congestion and wasteful consumption.

In a few years, it may seem obvious that the greatest asset of Eastern Canada is that it is not highly developed, that it still has forests, lakes, sea beaches and a relaxed way of life — just an hour or two away from the heaviest concentrations of population and industrialization in Canada and the United States.